Modern Samurai

Matt Stait

Modern Samurai

ISBN:9781789264500

Publisher: Independent publishing network

Copyright © 2018 by Matt Stait

All rights reserved. This book or any portion thereof may not be reproduced or used in any manner whatsoever without the express written permission of the author.

If you would like further information on talks, seminars, or workshops you can connect with me in the following ways:

www.modernsamurai.online

www.msma.academy

Facebook

LinkedIn

Instagram

Contents

Foreword 4

1: Introduction 6

2: New starters 17

3: There's a new sheriff in town 32

4: The night time economy 37

5: Drugs 58

6: The good, bad old days 75

7: Violence 87

8: Fame 103

9: The fairer sex 119

10: Sex and come-on's 132

11: Martial arts 149

12: You shouldn't laugh, but 170

13: After 186

Foreword

Having been asked to write a foreword for a book written by someone you know can result in a minor dilemma.

Do you become sycophantic and write wonderful words about the author and the book or do you simple be as honest as you can and write what you genuinely believe.

Given that l know Matt Stait to be a genuine and honest man, that l felt the only way to do this would be as honest as l could.

The Book is about Matts perception of his experiences 'on the doors', and it is an honest review of HIS and his fellow doormen of this vital and often misunderstood role.

Doormen are often portrayed as 'thugs' with a desire to 'beat people up', and it is hoped that the readers of this book will come to realise that very few genuine doormen will ever fall into these categories.

I have known Matt for many years as he and has martial arts club are members of my association. In fact, l am responsible for grading him for a couple of his black belts.

You will find Matt's honesty, humour and perception jumping out at you from the pages of this excellent book.

I heartily recommend this book for its insight and know you will thoroughly enjoy it and benefit from owing it.

David Turton 10th Dan

Head of the All Styles Martial Arts Association & the Self-Defence Federation

1: Introduction

The law is an ass

The law on self-defence as it is written down offers some fundamental points which state you can use reasonable force to protect yourself. What is reasonable to one however, may not be reasonable to another. Also, in a cold courtroom, 6 months, maybe a year down the line when you are surrounded by a bunch of legal types who have never had a fight in their lives acting as your judge, jury, and executioner what's reasonable is usually pretty bloody far removed from reality. I have stood in the dock as the accused and I have been there as a witness, I have always found it frustrating and I often wonder what world these people live in. It isn't mine that's for sure. At times like those I think let's put you on the door on a busy Saturday night with the rugby boys, gansta's, chemical heads and professional drinkers. Mr smart arse lawyer with your condescending tone and arrogant manner you would be either crying for your mum or lying in a pool of your own blood and teeth very quickly. You work in an environment where a clever turn of phrase or a barbed comment scores the point. We work in a world where the point could and is a broken beer bottle or a concealed knife or if you are really lucky, an infected syringe.

So, the word reasonable is subjective and you will be relying on other people with next to no experience of violence and violent people to look at you and decide, yes what you did was fine, we are not going to lock you up or take away your livelihood. Scary thought isn't it. But it is less scary than letting yourself be a victim for fear of the law. That way lies hospital beds and death. Your missus getting that knock on the door at silly o'clock with two uncomfortable looking pc's. Ones normally a woman in these situations so she can empathise. I have had that knock on the door and I did what any British person would do, I offered them a cup of tea.

People today won't stop after one punch with the words "you sir, are a cad". No, they will stamp on your head repeatedly; they will attack as a group like sharks in a feeding frenzy. People will stab, glass, bottle, bludgeon and bite you until you are a bloody pulp. One of the worst injuries I have seen was delivered by a petite young lady of about 20. A pretty little thing that was no more than 8 stone and I'm sure had a mum who loved her, but more on that later. The sad truth is that today our society is breaking down. Our police and emergency services are overstretched, overworked, and underpaid. Our legal system audibly groans under the sheer weight of numbers. Our leaders have no moral compass or backbone, our hero's and role models are flawed, selfish material beings and we have lost our way as a nation. With all this going on at the top is it any wonder that at the bottom, where I live and work, anarchy is only ever a drunken misunderstanding away. We cannot rely on people to be nice, so if you find yourself in a position where you must defend yourself. Do it, with no hesitation and 100% commitment. If you survive and come out the other end, then good, you have won that battle. If then you get arrested, then a whole new battle begins. One that must be fought through the courts, but if you don't survive the first battle the second one means nothing, so you should not let it cloud your thinking or make your actions hesitant. Working as a nightclub bouncer is like walking a tightrope. Sometimes it can be a fine line between survival and legal.

This is not a story of a "hard man". The pages are not full of bloodstained tales regaling the reader of the time I took on 20 Hell's Angels single handed or fought off the local drug gang using only my trusty SIA badge and a club stamp. Yes, there is violence in this book. Violence unfortunately goes with the job.

But there is also beauty, humour, camaraderie, highs and lows and many, many, boring hours on shift in between.

This is a true story in the sense that it paints a picture of my time on the doors, it's the ramblings of memory, remembering the characters, places and moments that stick in my mind. Some names, places and times have been changed to protect the innocent (and sometimes the guilty). I will leave it with you to decide what you believe.

I would like to think that you enjoy reading this as much as I did writing it. At times I have stopped typing, sat here, smiled, and remembered some of the faces and times over the years. The fun, the fights, the sometimes completely barmy situations, incredible people, and experiences that this job has given me. I would like to thank each and every one of them. Yes, even the dickheads for without them I would not have had a job.

Lastly, give a thought to the big ugly lump stood on the door the next time you are passing. We are not uneducated thugs. We are people, people who keep you and your loved ones safe at night. People who run towards while everyone else is running away. People who will save your kids from themselves while they get so wasted on drink and drugs that they can't remember their own name. Without us clubland would be a very different place.

Acknowledgements:

I would like to thank the following people. There are many more, and I would like to thank you all but that would be a book, albeit a very boring one.

My mum who has supported me throughout and brought my sister and I up in the 70's when times were hard. It's only now years later that I can begin to understand the personal sacrifice and hardships you must have endured.

My dad who left us far too young. There are so many things I would have liked to have said. I hope that you are proud of me.

Bob, for helping to make possibilities realities.

Kath Hill. This was her maiden name, she has since married. When I was a young man 18 or so I used to sing in a rock band. I was pretty crap but every band practise Kath would collect me and drive me there. I always said back then I would acknowledge her on my first album. Surprise, surprise we never got signed. So here we are over 20 years later fulfilling a promise. Sorry it wasn't on an album Kath.

Lastly, all of my extended martial arts and door family. I am lucky to have had many inspirational people in my life. They continue to help, inspire, and support me. Thank you to all of you, you cannot imagine how important this have been to my life and I feel blessed that you would take the time to share your knowledge with me. Special thanks to all my instructors past or present, without your guidance and knowledge I would not be what I am today. You all have taught me so much and I could never fully repay the debt. I am amazed and truly grateful that this spotty faced kid from a small town who spent many years reading about all these great people and watching them in awe has had the opportunity to travel to far off countries and to meet and train with so many of my heroes.

Who am I?

My name is Matt Stait and I started learning martial arts in the late eighties. At first it was a hobby I dropped in and out of. It had been a deep-down dream of mine that one day I would be like the stars of the screen, knocking over bad guys like pins in a bowling alley and fearing no man. But back then I had neither the willpower or belief to carry out the many years of study to gain the skills required to do that. I had been bullied as a child and felt capitulation was my only answer. Well one day my father committed suicide, and everything changed. Just like that my world would forever be a different place. I bounced around for a bit, got drunk and partied, made wrong choices, and generally became a waste of space. Sacked from one dead end job to another and hanging around accomplishing nothing. This had to stop so one day I walked into a Karate dojo and the real transformation began.

I saw a whole new world of manhood, you didn't need to growl at everyone or have bar fights and be a bully to be a man. You could be a softly spoken, articulate and a likeable guy and still be able to switch on this other side of yourself when required. This was a revelation to me. Here were people who looked average right up until the point when they moved. It was like watching a snake strike or a lioness bring down her prey. This latent physicality lay dormant within them giving no sign to the outside world what lurked just beneath the surface. But in the dojo, where the mind and body were hardened on hour after hour of painful repetition, you saw the weapon being forged and the blade sharpened. Hour after hour, day after day, night after night. Days became weeks and weeks became years. Over 25 years have passed since those early beginnings and in that time I have fought competitively becoming a world champion gold silver and bronze medallist, gained multiple black belts and instructor licenses, been inducted into the MIA blackbelt hall of fame, moved into self-defence and combatives and run a full time martial arts gym, I also teach in schools up and down the country and deliver the training required to work in security.

While on that journey I worked in security. For many years my days would be spent on the building sites and my evenings going from pubs to clubs, events, festivals, concerts, student balls, close protection, and asset protection. I have covered just about every role from head doorman to pit crew to cp to covert security to debt collector to retail to event management and ops manager. I have stood on city centre clubs and casino's, small town working men's clubs, gay bars, rock clubs, corporate functions, festivals and just about everything in between. This eventually led to me ditching the building sites and going full-time. Now as a practising martial artist for many years. I teach self-defence to groups and organisations. I go to schools along with the charity Stand against Violence and educate the kids. I deliver SIA approved courses including conflict management and physical intervention to the security industry. I am an author and online trainer. Does any of this make me an expert? No, but it does make for some interesting stories.

But all this is in the future, at the start I was a tall gangly kid unsure but willing to learn. I used to go to work wearing jumpers under my shirt to make me look bigger. I used to hope no-one would notice. And I never did become the hero in the movie. I was always afraid, I just learned to handle it better

Introduction Part 2

I was born in the November of 1970 in a place called the Royal Gwent Hospital in Newport, South Wales. This is a large grey foreboding set of buildings that oozes with the suffering of its history. The staff I am sure were great. I was too young to remember but the building remains, cheerless and brooding. I was the oldest so was the first. We didn't have a lot of money and things were tight. My mother bought us up alone and worked full time. I remember being dragged from house to house as a kid so that she could collect the pools money. I've no idea how she managed to feed and clothe us, but she did, though I wasn't always happy with what was supplied. Going to school in ugly steel toe capped shoes because mum could get them from work for free when everyone else was sporting the latest Nikes used to really piss me off. I still have nightmares about a particular pair of green corduroy flares.

We moved around a bit in my childhood years, mostly in various areas of south Wales. The town I grew up in was a place called Chepstow, a beautiful market town, situated on the border between England and Wales. Before the curse of the supermarket chains blighted it, Chepstow was a vibrant little town with a busy high street and a famous Sunday market. The castle looms over the whole town and we were surrounded by some of the most beautiful countryside that the U.K. has to offer. There were many local pubs and bars but in those days they all shut at 11.30pm. Today things are different, and a lot of these places have closed and been turned into flats, but these were my first experiences of going out and I have many happy memories. As a young man I found the small-town way of life constricting and wanted to see and experience other places, to have adventures filled with excitement and beautiful women but I didn't have the balls to go out and get them.

Then one day my father committed suicide. I often ask myself why, but I never did find an answer. I suddenly had to grow up and although I regret deeply the path he chose, if he had not have done that I may well have spent the rest of my life living a life I wasn't happy with. Destined to marry the girl down the road and work for forty-five years in a job I hated, living for the weekend when I could drink the disappointment away. So that day turned out to be both the best and the worst day of my life. My dad was a larger than life guy that I worshipped, and I miss him even now. But that day forced me to change, to step out into the world and become my own man.

After bumming around for a while I ended up in Bristol, which has been my home for the past twenty something years. I love this city with its quirky architecture and underground music scene., the history of the place is evident wherever you go and a walk through the docks after a shift at 6am on a Sunday morning is a real joy. The people are down to earth, slightly reserved but great and loyal friends when you get to know them. The constant hum of all the people going about their lives and something going on twenty-four seven, with the sounds of seagulls and sirens lulling you to sleep when you finally go to bed.

This is where it all began amongst the universities and the landmarks, the night life, the clubs and bars and of course our world-famous graffiti.

2: New starters

What does it take to be a bouncer these days? Do you have to be big? Do you have to be a martial arts expert, or a boxer? Do you need a "rep" as the local hard man?

No, you don't, not anymore. Now all you need is a four-day course and a little plastic badge and there you go, as if by magic you are now a fully-fledged, ready for anything kick ass, cool as a mutha-fucka door supervisor.

This is the unfortunate state you find our industry in in these modern times. Since the introduction of the SIA the face of club security and doormen and women has changed, and not entirely for the better in my humble opinion. Once upon a time to be a doorman meant something, you were there because you could do the job, you were the enforcer before cctv and police radios. If there was a problem at your venue, you dealt with it. If not.... well, you found another line of work. Being able to handle yourself was a necessity back in those days and if you couldn't "have a row" then you would soon be found out by your team and promptly told to politely go away. This was before everyone dressed as para militaries with their combats, viper belt and detachable pouches. We wouldn't have been seen dead in a hi-vis. The dress code was smart, with a crisp white shirt and a dickie bow. Underneath that was the aura, the way they carried themselves with confidence and the knowledge of battles won. That persona that they could rise to any challenge presented. I hoped one day that I would look like that.

Nowadays as I walk around the city I despair of some of the sights I see. Chewing gum and trying to talk like Clint Eastwood does not make you a bad-ass. Dressing like you are going to replay the Iranian embassy siege does not turn you into a one-man SAS unit. There are still a lot of very good and capable doormen/women out there protecting our clubbers, but we have been swamped with jacket fillers and wannabes who quite honestly, I wouldn't trust to collect trolleys in a supermarket carpark.

I had a conversation a few years back with an old friend who I used to knock about with but have since lost touch. After not seeing him for many years we bumped into each other and we got talking. Our lives had taken very different paths and while I spent every free moment studying the martial arts he had gone on to be a force within the local football hooligan scene. He asked what I was doing these days and when I explained that I was working the doors he pulled a bit of a face and then proceeded to tell me about the rows him and his boys had had with security over the years. The upshot of this conversation was that he said he had no real respect for bouncers any more as it wasn't like the old days. He said most of them couldn't fight and were there for decoration only. He went on to say years previously you didn't hit a doorman, and if you did you expected a good hiding there and then. If you jumped a doorman you would expect a team visit as they all stuck together. Police were rarely involved, and the respect was there. Not any more he said. "There is no fear anymore". The old school ways are fading out and becoming nothing but memories.

Before the introduction of the license to become a doorman what usually happened is you knew someone who would put you forward for a shift. If you were ok and didn't mess up, you would be asked if you wanted to do another. Over time after proving yourself you would become part of the team where the shift didn't end with the words do you want a shift next week? But instead we will see you next week. All this took time. Now someone can do a short course and be put in charge of a large venue with lots of people. After a few days you can be paid the same as someone with 10 years under their belt.

But things are not all bad. Since the introduction of the SIA changes have been brought about to stop the criminality in the security industry. Measures have been put in place to weed out certain people and practises including drugs and violence. The darker side of life was running rampant and needed to be curbed. Does this still go on? I'm sure it must. There will always be a minority but to be fair to the SIA in the main they have stamped it out and brought about a much more professional industry. Here's hoping that one day the wages will catch up and reflect that.

So, a training and monitoring system was introduced, first the old council licenses and then the infamous SIA badge. To achieve enough to possess one of these all you need do is a four-day course which covers only the very basics. It may surprise you to learn if you are not from the industry that until 2012 it wasn't compulsory to have any form of physical intervention training. Now we have a raft of different providers offering the necessary training which is done in a day and a half and teaches non-pain compliant tactics and very low-level restraints. Yes, I deliver this course as part of my working life and I like to think that the system I teach is one of the better ones out there but the truth of it is we are hamstrung by the guidelines of the course content. We are forced to present the most effective training we can following the SIA remit. This means that although I believe in what I teach it will only get you so far. If, and when an 18-stone rugby player decides to tap dance on your head, that shit is not going to save you.

Get yourself some proper training. Take yourself off to martial arts or boxing or even a good game of rugby. Anything that involves contact and getting used to being physical. It's not like the classroom, not everyone will quietly walk away after you have told them" the rules" in your stern voice. There are people out there that will beat you a new head at best so take my advice and go learn some skills. We have a strange industry right now where kids barely old enough to legally enter licensed premises and have never had a fight in their lives are tasked with policing a venue and dealing with everything the night time economy can throw at them.

If you hired an electrician to come and do some work at your home, you would expect him to be able to wire a plug. Yet we are now sending out people with absolutely no experience to deal with violent people and sometimes quite extreme situations. How are these guys and girls going to look after you and your loved ones if the nearest they have ever been to a real fight is watching the UFC on the telly and practising their no-nonsense bouncer face in the mirror?

Nowadays we have so many people coming into the industry as a way to earn a living, not everyone is suited to the job. Totally unsuitable people can now get a license for free from the dole office and every other eight stone student thinks it pays better than bar work. We've got good guys and girls coming through as well, people that want to help others and better their life. Over the years I've seen many people come and go, some because it was a stop gap for them, a way to finance an education or to see them through to the promotion and welcome pay rise. Some choose the job because of their life style; the hours suit them, and they can spend the day with the kids. Others to massage their ego or to give themselves a name or a reputation. Whatever the reason for choosing door work only a few were ever really suited to it. Like a dog chasing a bus! Yes, the dog is trying to catch the bus, but it has no clue what the hell to do with it. This is true with a lot of the newbies today. Be careful what you wish for because it might come true.

I will introduce you to some of the new starters I have met. Some good, some not.

The first guy we will call Peter. I've changed the names of people and places throughout this book to protect the innocent. And sometimes guilty! There will be people that recognise themselves within these pages and all I can say is "if you think it's you, it probably is." If I describe you in an unflattering light, then I am sorry. You shouldn't have acted like a dick. People's perceptions of an event or person can be skewed through drink and/or drugs and for a lot of people that overwhelming fear of admitting that they are wrong. Every minute of every shift I have ever worked I have done so stone cold sober, so if I offend anyone, sorry but this is how I saw it and it's my book. If you remember things differently, then write your own.

Working for a security company usually means you get sent to different venues and places depending on what contracts they have. This particular job was to work overnight and look after a load of marquees. Not very glamorous I know and usually very boring work. The upside to this was that it was a thirteen-hour shift which meant good money and the view.

The marquees were for a centenary celebration for a local private school. Not just any school mind you. This place looked like Hogwarts and cost a fortune to enrol in. A lot of the good and the great had been here and this weekend they were celebrating that fact. The buildings are hundreds of years old and surround a courtyard which looks out over the grounds. This is how the other half live. Although my life was never privileged enough to have ever gone to one of these places for a few hours I could enjoy the beauty and history that ten thousand pound a term could bring. My job for the night was to deter anyone wandering into the grounds and to stop the local urban foxes from getting into the catering tent. Here I was to meet a guy called Peter who was going to be my partner for the night. So, a car pulls up and a short middle-aged man gets out. He was Eastern European but spoke English well and was wearing the full outfit. I mean everything. The army surplus boots and combat trousers, the webbing belt, bomber jacket and slash proof gloves. As he walked towards me and outstretched his Kevlar gloved hand to shake, I though this guy is a bit over the top but after greeting me what he said next totally blew me away. As he was pulling at his bat-belt with various attachable Velcro pouches, he told me that he had bought with him a pair of night vision goggles which he then proceeded to pull out and proudly wave in front of me. Well that was it for me. There was no way I could take him seriously from then on. Talk about overkill. Do you really need all of that to look after a tent and maybe if we got really lucky, chase a mangy fox away? I never saw Peter again after that shift and sometimes I wonder if he is in a Morrisons somewhere whispering into his sleeve and hiding behind the cornflakes, staking out suspicious shoppers. He didn't belong on a door.

Another guy that immediately springs to mind we will call Tim. Now Tim was a fine figure of a man standing 6ft 6ins tall with big arms and broad shoulders tapered off to a tucked in waistline gained through years of university rowing. The women must have swooned at this guy and to be honest he must have been strong and very fit to compete in such an intensive sport. I met Tim at a festival in South Wales. A relatively small event catering for families and locals with a capacity of around two thousand. It was a beautiful summer's day and the sun was shining down, so we were all in tee shirts and sun glasses as we were allocated our positions ready for opening. There were two entrances to the site, one at the top where the public would come in and another at the bottom of the site for vendors, artists etc. It was decided that as it was Tim's first security shift he would be placed at the back entrance for the first part of the day as it would be quiet, and he would have the chance to settle in without it being too demanding for him. So, the day began, and the gates opened and slowly but consistently the punters started arriving, excited at the prospect of being entertained in an all too rare sunshiny summer's day. These nice people had all bought tickets to get in and were prepared with picnics, deck chairs, blankets, sun cream and bag loads of other paraphernalia. Our job was to welcome them in, check tickets and to make sure that anything that was not supposed to be coming in was left outside. We had our search table set up and spent the morning light heartedly telling middle aged couples off for trying to sneak in a bread knife in the picnic basket and having general banter with the customers. The mood was jovial, as these things almost always are at the start of the day. but as the day wears on and alcohol starts to flow there will always be people to spoil it. So, the inevitable happened and our first idiot of the day shows up. He was a local guy known to the police in the area, he had a drug habit, bad attitude, and terrible personal hygiene. Unlike the nice people we had dealt with so far, this fellow decided that buying a ticket was not an option, but he still wanted to enjoy the day and maybe shark a few half empty cans from unsuspecting locals. He decided the best way to achieve this was to sneak in through the bottom entrance. The one on which Tim had been placed. So, this rather smelly jumble sale on legs attempts to jump the fence near to the back gate when he is spotted and challenged by Tim.

Now we are all animals, albeit clothed and usually civilised but some of us more animal than others. This guy being feral could smell the uncertainty from Tim and knew despite his size he could be intimidated. So, that is what he did. He told Tim he was going to stab him if he didn't let him go in so that is exactly what Tim did. Let him go, straight in the festival. We received a call over the radio and immediately went to respond, running through the now thickening groups of families that had pitched up and snaking through the burger vans and other vendors touting for business. When we got to Tim he had removed his hi-viz and quit on the spot. He quietly handed it over with his radio and walked off to his car. Although he never saw a knife the threat was enough to scare him into leaving. I have never seen him again and assume that he decided that security work wasn't for him. The kid with the drug habit was picked up ten minutes later and escorted away by the Police. It turned out that although physically he seemed built for the job, mentally and emotional he wasn't. I've lost count of the times over the years I've been threatened with being stabbed. It's a lot. Maybe I just have one of those faces.

The next guy I will introduce to you is a disturbing case. I don't know if he was a new DS (door supervisor) or just new to our company, but I know he hadn't been on the doors long. We shall call this guy Uncle Fester. Obviously not his real name but that is what we christened him. Whenever he is mentioned it is by that name. At the time I first became aware of this guy I was covering security at a city centre hotel so would often be found gazing out of the window at all the late-night stupidity. It was a one-man door, so the hours rolled past very slowly unless something was happening in the hotel. From midnight onwards, Bristol City Centre was better than the television for seeing people do some strange things. Once or twice I had noticed this guy all dressed up in his doorman attire with his license strapped to his arm walking around the city. I assumed he had a venue to go to but now I not so sure. Over a few weekends we got to nodding as he went by. Then a brief hello and after a few weeks sometimes he would stop to chat. This never lasted long as I was never keen on the guy and something did not sit right with me. After a few weeks of this he ended up on our firm, bought in by a friend of a friend, sort of thing. He was put on one of the local gay bars which was also a one-man door. Here is where his story started to unravel. During a shift he got involved with an argument with a couple and ended up punching the guy. This disagreement came around because the female had accused him of attempting to rape her previously. We didn't find this out until later. Then a few days later at another small venue the management reported that the guy had been asked not to come back as he had allegedly tried to sexually assault one of the female patrons on the stairs by the toilets. He was immediately dismissed from the firm and his details passed to the relevant authorities. It was after this second incident that we found out that he did not have a previous venue on the weekends that I saw him. Yet, he was walking around in security logos and wearing his badge. We reached the conclusion that what he was doing was using this to get to vulnerable women late at night, pretending to hold a position of authority, as a cover for anyone watching and to gain the trust of his intended victims. I have never seen or heard of this type of thing before or since and this is why the SIA was bought in to stop these sorts of people being allowed to work in security. All security companies on the approved contractor's scheme must vet every member of staff and they all must have a checkable work history. This does mean that the companies involved incur extra costs but for Joe Public it ensures a safer and more accountable staff and will hopefully put a stop to people like Uncle Fester. Those were some pretty negative examples of new starters but it's not all bad. Its's been my privilege to work with and mentor some really good guys.

Meet Dan. He came to me fresh out of the box, nineteen years old and his first ever shift was with me. Stan trained as a brickie but the early mornings, cold days and the recession made him think twice about his career choices. So, he went and got his badge. A friend of his father who worked as a DS recommended him to the company, so he was given a shot. Quite often during my time with this particular firm I would be sent new starters to assess them and to see if they were worth keeping and to train them in the right way so that they would become an asset to the team. The venue at the time was called Underground 69 (name change) but anyone who has ever been there will recognise it. I was the head doorman. This venue usually opened around 10pm and stayed open until 4am playing dub step, drum and bass and other variations of that thumping, monotonous genre. It is situated down some stairs just of the main strip nicknamed the waterfalls because that is where everyone went for a late-night piss. It would trickle down the steps like a waterfall. The club itself boasts two dance floors and a capacity that was regularly ignored by management at the time. The music was loud and there were no windows so when it was busy the sweat would drip from the low ceilings. The clientele ranged in ages from eighteen to thirty and dressed down, this was all joggers and baseball caps with a large order of attitude. Drugs were rife, and the scene was full of drug culture and ASBO kids looking to spend their dole money. In the early days you were guaranteed at least one fight a night. Nice people did come in, but they were in the minority. The number of unworldly students we saved from their own stupidity must be massive. There were usually three DS on a weekend, sometimes four if it was busy so we needed a tight team. Everyone had to carry their own weight. This venue had the ability to get ugly very quickly and needed a firm control policy. Fortunately, the manager and owner at the time was a man who understood this and supported his security team all the way, which is a rarity these days. This is the place were Dan got started on his door career.

It was a normal weekend and I had turned up at the venue. I was going through the pre-opening check list and getting ready for the busy night ahead when Dan turned up. He stood around 6ft tall with a large frame, wider in the middle, than at the shoulders. He had a young face with a cheeky smile, which he tried to hide with a short fuzzy beard. He had a background in judo and a collection of tap out tee shirts, plus a willing to learn attitude that I liked. So, I got him signed in and showed him around. And then we begin our shift. He did well on that first day and became a mainstay on the team, following me to other venues when I took over at those. We faced many difficult situations together and never once have I looked over my shoulder running into something and he wasn't there right behind me. He never turned down a shift and was always professional and even tempered with the clients. He's still on the firm and makes a fairly good living from it. We will meet Dan again later in the book and hear some of the stories we shared.

So, these are just a few of the many new starters I have meet over the years and now as I'm creeping into middle age I think it is approaching time to let the new guys and girls carry on with it. Every year we have a new batch of uni students coming in and every couple of years the next generation of the problem families become old enough to bring their mischief to my door. I have witnessed this cycle many times over now; as I'm getting older these guys stay the same. New faces but doing the same stupid shit. Every generation thinks they are the first to discover partying. That's the natural order of things and I have watched over them as they have fought, fucked, got fucked and fucked over each other and my faith in human nature and my patience is waning. For you new guys and girls it's a massive adventure full of excitement and colourful characters and I wish you well on your journey and hope you stay safe.

3: There's a new sheriff in town

My first ever night working came about from a chance conversation and to be honest was quite unremarkable apart from one small thing. If you have seen or heard of the film Sliding Doors in which fate dictates the path of your life and follows the outcomes. This night was very similar. I had been training in martial arts for quite a while and winning a few competitions here and there and got chatting to a guy I knew who worked the doors. He asked myself and another lad if we fancied a shift. This was back in the day and you were paid in cash, well that sounded great to me. A few extra quid, and a night checking out the local talent. Yes, I said, that would be great. The next night or two was spent working on my 'doorman face' in the mirror and fantasising about all the good-looking women that were going to throw themselves at me. I wasn't scared so much as nervous, but from the moment I agreed to this the little whirring in the pit of my stomach was a constant companion and my sleep was engulfed in dreams of every movie fight scene I had ever watched, with me as the victor obviously. (I Shouldn't have bothered with those dreams as real-world violence looks nothing like the choreographed dance you see on screen). I'm sure that the other lad must have gone through a similar build up as unknown to me at the time that was my body slow releasing adrenaline and those reactions are perfectly normal.

Anyway, Saturday night arrived and while the rest of the country prepared to go out and get drunk I found myself putting on my newly brought doorman's outfit. The first time I put it on I looked at myself in the mirror and thought I look scrawny so off I went to find a jumper to put under my shirt. It will make me look bigger I reasoned and I just hoped I could make it through the night without anyone finding out my weedy little secret. Off we went to the rendezvous, myself and this other lad, to be met and told we would be working at separate venues. Bugger! I hadn't anticipated that as he was my emotional crutch, my only friend amongst all of this. Suddenly I felt very alone and began to question if this was really for me. Like a lot of people, the thought of being a bouncer can seem pretty enticing, when you're there and it's happening, well that's a little different.

So, I found myself at this pretty unremarkable edge of town pub/club alongside two other doorstaff who seemed a little reserved towards me but also seemed to know their stuff. Over the years I found myself treating the new starters the same way, earn the respect of your colleagues and then they open up. Nothing much happened to me that first evening, no mass brawls or even a single fight. We took out a few drunks and turned a few away at the door with no real hassle, but I must have done ok because at the end of the night I was asked back.

My new start partner on the other hand had a different tale to tell. He had also been sent to a venue similar to mine but with one extra ds. Around the middle of the evening as the queue was starting to build two lads approached. Dressed to impress but not actually impressive they expectantly walked towards the door." Not tonight lads" were the words spoken as an arm was raised chest height blocking their path. "why not?" was there instant reply, said in a slightly challenging tone. My friend had no part in this conversation as he was following the lead of the more experienced guys so just stood slightly off to the side watching. "Because you were thrown out last week for fighting mate, that's why" said doorman number one. "The boss says you're barred" he added. Straight away the two lads went from zero to hero. "Who the fuck do you think you are to tell us what to do? Don't you know who we are? We are gunna fuck yo........"

At which point the doorman number one pushed the chopsy kid backwards with a well-practised doorman shove. The kid flew back skating on invisible ice and landed in pile six feet away while his mate double stepped back out of range and had that confused I Don't know what to do next look on his face. He was fine giving it all the talk before it went physical and he had his mate for moral support but now with his mate led on his back with his legs in the air things were different. The lad on the floor wasn't happy and bounced right back up. Realising that physical was going to get him hurt he resorted to the next best thing when you find yourself in that situation. Stand ten yards back and threaten the dreaded comeback. "I'm going to get the boys and fucking do you! You are gonna get fucking shot! I will be back, and we are gonna fuck you up!" With that him and his mate wandered off into the night with the sound of threats still echoing through the air. The small queue went back to shuffling into the club and after a few murmurs things were back to normal. For the punters here, this sort of thing happened a lot and was not news. Neither was it news for the ds. They had heard it all before, many times and so they reassured my slightly rattled friend. " Pair of numbnuts mate, lots of shouting but they don't have the bollocks to do anything like that. We hear this shit all the time and 99% of it is just talk, trying to make themselves feel better after the knockback".

Things settled a little and the incident was put to the back of his mind. Back to the monotony of checking id's and making sure nobody was too drunk to come in. As he was asking a young lady for her date of birth the question was interrupted by the sound of screeching tyres, an over-revved engine and worst of all loud bangs. Women screamed and flung themselves to the floor, I'm pretty sure my mate screamed too, although he denies it. The lads from earlier were back, only this time they had some friends and were in a Ford Sierra firing an air rifle. After firing off a shot and throwing a few half bricks out the window they sped off into the night. My mate and his partner stood up and checked themselves over. Luckily nothing had hit them and although completely rattled by the incident they were otherwise unscathed.

That was the one and only shift my mate ever did on the doors. He said never again and if the tables were turned and I had gone through that I also would have never set foot on another door. But it wasn't me that it happened to, so I took the next shift, and the one after that and before too long I was working and living the doorman lifestyle.

4: The night time economy

I was once told or read somewhere, I can't quite remember that nothing good ever happens after midnight. I can't say if this is true but it's definitely true to say a lot of the "nicer "elements of our customers disappear before the clock strikes 12. The name of the game is to sell alcohol in all its different forms to anyone with money to spend. The offers and promotions are there to lure people to the venue and the venue is designed to create an atmosphere where you will part with your hard-earned cash. Happy hours and 2 for 1 deals are everywhere, drink vouchers and discounted entry with this flyer hammer the message home that this club is the place to be seen. Certain areas of towns and cities all over the country are famous for their bars and clubs and Bristol is no different, with a venue to suit all types from famous chain pubs with its cheap and cheerful approach where old men gum their Guinness and the most expensive thing on the menu is £2.50 through to the high end cocktail bars where wannabe z list celebs hang out and the girls squeeze into dresses two sizes too small with skin the colour of a cheesy wotsit. They are all very different in their approach, but all are trying to do the same thing, take your money.

The average wage of a club bouncer is about £10 per hour, for festival work and concerts £9, shop security is even less at £8. For that you face serious injury and criminal proceedings against you every single shift you work. The money has not gone up for many years and in fact that is what we used to be paid in cash when I started. Some of us through experience and reputation demand and deserve a higher rate of pay but no amount of money will recompense you or your family if you are seriously hurt or locked up.

The club wants to pay as little as possible for its outgoings so staffing costs are a big issue. Security firms via for the contracts with less and less profit margins and the festival scene is flooded with sub-contracted workers four to five people down the employment chain. If you are lucky you will find a good firm to work for. If you do, show them loyalty as they are rare. It is very common now to find you are on a zero-hour contract that states you cannot work for anyone else. No holiday or sick pay and in what is a legally grey area some companies are demanding you pay for you own uniforms and then charge you for insurance as well. My advice is to find the best company that you can and stick with them.

We are tasked with holding that impossible line between too drunk to come in and a manager that wants to hit his targets, so he can collect his bonus. So, let's start there, with the drunk customer. Any doorman that has ever worked has had the conversation and it goes like this. "not tonight mate, your drunk". Punter replies with "no, I'm not". This then turns into a 20-minute debate with the disgruntled customer repeating over and over that they are not drunk, in fact even though it is eleven thirty on a Saturday night and they look as if they are standing in a force nine gale they have only drank one pint all night. Usually they become very indignant and demand that we must let them in as they are in no way inebriated and will usually try to prove it by going into the pantomime of the American police dui stop. "Look", they cry," I can touch my nose. Let me walk an imaginary tightrope for you. I'm standing on one leg, so I must be sober". And it goes on and on, depending on the sort of person you're dealing with sometimes it's amusing but mostly it's very irritating and none of it will change the decision once it's been made.

Criminality is rife after dark and crime has an economy all of its own. From the street thieves to the ticket touts, the drug dealers and sex workers to the organised pickpocketing gangs. Everybody is trying to make a few quid.

The doorman shove.

When it comes to running a club or a bar, security is crucial. How you choose your team can make or break a club. The problem with a good team though is that it looks like it's doing nothing. When the security is doing a good job hardly anything ever happens because they have usually stopped it before it started or dealt with the problem quickly. This can then lead the management to think that they can get the job done for cheaper and the undercutting between rival firms begins. That extra pound an hour saving on the wages bill suddenly starts looking good but here's an example of the real cost.

I'm driving down to London, I come here to deliver training on a reasonably regular basic and had trained quite a few hospital security teams down this way, but this one was different. I managed to find the club and park and then made my way to the side doors where a few guys where hanging around smoking. They pointed through the doorway and down a corridor, so I went in the direction shown and found myself in a large bar area laid out with classroom style tables and chairs. I was going to be supporting with the physical training of the club staff today and was met by the other trainer for the day who was the owner of the training company and he filled me in on what had happened.

Rob is one of those characters you meet sometimes, and he is just a lot to take in. I remember being a little confrontational with him when we first met as back then I thought he had a touch of the used car salesman about him. Now, he genuinely is one of my favourite people and I always enjoy doing the training course with him as he is such a livewire and very knowledgeable. Normally your first view of him is out the front fag in hand, pacing. He drinks red bull at an alarming rate and his energy levels would wear out a coke head. He was a doorman for many years down Bournemouth way and is very passionate about what he does and that comes through in his teaching methods. I always learn a lot when I work with him and today would be no exception.

We were in probably the biggest live music club in London which had a security team of nearly thirty, all of which were having to undergo the training we were providing. Two weeks earlier there had been an incident and a young girl had been hurt. I was told that this girl had been having an issue with the door team. This had carried on for over twenty minutes and escalated to the point where the girl was trying to scratch her nails into one of the doorman's faces, so he shoved her back out of reach. Unfortunately, the young lady staggered back and impaled herself on some iron railings with the force of the push. The local community were very unhappy with this situation and things became very heated. Lots of things were said and death threats were made over social media. The club owners and staff were in genuine fear and the club had to be shut down for a period. It was decided that for the club to reopen a completely new CCTV system had to be installed and the remaining security team had to be retrained to an improved standard. The cost of the club being closed in ongoing overheads and lost revenue must have been huge. Then add the cost of all the new equipment and required training. Then add in the cost of the good will of the community and the bill is enormous. A good door supervisor is worth every penny because the cost of a bad one is staggering.

How to double your money.

Once you had been working a while and your reputation started to get known other opportunities would present themselves. If you were a certain sort of person you could make money in a lot of different ways. In the evenings I would work the doors, through the summer we would do the festival circuit and in between this I would pick up odd jobs here and there not all of them entirely legal.

I was approached by a guy called Steve. He had moved down from the north and was a manager of a homeless hostel. It's strange but if you lined him up with the clientele you probably wouldn't know one from the other. Steve had a hippy girlfriend who had wide hips and loved those long flowery skirts. Together they liked to spend their evenings smoking weed and listening to music. One evening while smoking and listening to Pink Floyd they had hatched a plan to make some extra money.

Through a common friend I agreed to meet Steve and listen to what he was offering, so we met in one of those chain coffee shops and talked it over. He was on a salary and he claimed that he was underpaid and that it did not give him the lifestyle he wanted. What he intended to do every month was take that salary and buy a lump sum of weed. He would then portion it up and distribute it at a profit literally doubling his money. The only problem he could see was that he was vulnerable for that time and certain people may try to take it away from him. What he wanted from me is that I would escort him to the buy and then stick with him until drop off acting as a deterrent and taking care of any problems that arose. For this he was offering me good cash money. Now I know that what he was doing was illegal and I'm aware that morally it may not have been the right choice, but I took the job as I had bills to pay of my own. The money offered was good and all I had to really do was follow him around.

I was stood at the end of the street as the car pulled up, I opened the door and got into the passenger seat and said hi to Steve. It was payday, and this was going to be our first run. He had cashed his pay check and had a months' worth of wages in cash in his pocket. He was hyper and waffled non-stop during the journey. I zoned him out and inspected the crap car we were in; the ashtray was full of dogends and the passenger footwell was strewn with McDonalds wrappers and empty monster cans. This was not the transport of a drug dealer, but it was his first time. We drove across the city and out into one of the council estates. Trainers dangled from the wires that run above the streets, the road signs had all been defaced to stop people finding their way around and groups of kids loitered together staring at us as we drove past. We pulled up outside this council house that looked exactly the same as every other house we had passed on the estate. Out the front was a caravan half covered in a ratty tarpaulin and a large German

Shepard barked and paced behind a metal gate. On entering the front room, we were told to sit down, I took a chair and looked around. The guy we were speaking to was local. He had a thick Bristolian accent and Bristol city football club tattoos on his arm. The room itself looked normal if a little downtrodden, again I found myself asking if this was the lifestyle of a drug dealer. Before long the deal was done, and Steve and I left with a large amount of weed in a Tesco's carrier bag. I shoved it under the passenger seat as we made the journey back to Steve's rented flat where his hippy missus was waiting to greet us. It took them about an hour to portion it all out. They had a little system going so the drugs were weighed, measured, and bagged in no time at all. A few phone calls were made and once again we are back in the car with a large quantity of weed under the seat. We made a few stops along the way, never actually leaving the car. Steve's contacts would appear from pub doorways or rush out the communal stairwells of high rise flats and greet him through the car window. Sometimes I would get acknowledged, mostly they would just look at me for a second and then carry on. This was all done reasonably openly and although it was low key it was obvious what was happening. After the last drop off was done we made our way back to the flat. I sat on the couch drinking a coffee and watched as he emptied his pockets and threw the wads of notes onto the table. He stacked and counted them making neat little piles with the different denominations. We he had finished he had over double his monthly salary sat in front of him in cash. The whole process from being picked up on the street corner till now had taken about five hours. We did this every month for a while and I never once had to lift a finger or be physical with anyone, all I did was sat in the car and listened to the stupid stories he would tell.

Morals. They are expensive.

He introduced himself as Harry, he was about fifty and balding. He was dressed in a cheap suit and was fidgeting non-stop. He was sat opposite me constantly chewing on his fingernails and rapid firing sentences at me as fast as he could think of them. We were in my front room which had a dining area attached and in that space was a table and chairs. We sat on the chairs facing one another, on the table between us was a list of case files. These were people who owed money and Harry was in full swing trying to recruit me as a debt collector. The deal was very simple, these were people who for whatever reason hadn't paid their debts and for a percentage of what was owed I would recover it. If I couldn't get the money back I made nothing. This is a murky world and it was quite a few years ago now. It wasn't illegal as such but some of the practises people used certainly were.

It started off reasonably well. I was at a house, on the windowsills were rows of figurines and photo frames that were subjected to regular polishing, the garden was well manicured, and a tidy mid-level saloon car sat on the drive. We were in a reasonable area of a small town and I had knocked the door a few times with no answer. The lady owed money, over £800 in unpaid bills which judging by the house she could pay if she chose to. I saw one of the neighbours doing some gardening so used the opportunity to fish for some information. It turns out the lady and her husband were on holiday in Spain at that very moment and were expected back a week Tuesday. Well a week Tuesday I was back and recovered the money and felt pretty ok about it. Unfortunately though, not every job was as black and white.

This was a guy whose debts had spiralled and were now in the thousands. His file showed me a man in his late thirties who worked as a builder and originally had a few assets. However, he had proved hard to track down and according to my information had been unresponsive and uncooperative in trying to fix the problem. That was now my job. The current address I had for him was his mother's house and so that is where I stood. I had rung the bell and I was waiting. The door opened, and a very short older lady stared up at me not saying a word. I introduced myself and asked to come in where I was shown to the living room and sat down. At the side of the room pushed against the wall was a single bed and in the bed was the builder I had come to find. His mum put the kettle on and made a cup of tea while I listened to his story. He had been a reasonably successful builder, not loads of money but enough to pay the bills and have a few pints on the weekend. He hadn't been very good with managing it though as mostly the working class were never shown how to look after cash and so it was very much in one hand, out the other. This was fine for many years as there was always more coming in than going out.

One day while on the way home from a job his van had a blowout and skidded across two lanes of the motorway, it clipped a wagon and flipped. Completely rolling over twice before coming to a stop. He lay on his side strapped into the seat with the warm sticky blood puddled around him waiting for the ambulance and fire brigade. Eventually they cut him out and rushed him to the hospital where he underwent extensive surgery to save his life. His rehabilitation so far had taken eighteen months and over twenty operations. He could stand and walk three to four paces unaided, but no-one knew if he would ever be able walk properly again. Obviously during this time he had been unable to work and had lost his home and assets. What insurances he did have in place were trying their best to find ways to stall and not pay out while our benefit system that you hope would come to your aid at a time like this had actually just been a faceless wall of bureaucracy that just compounded all his other problems. All this had led to him ending up trapped in a makeshift bed in his elderly mother's front room with people like me hounding him for money he clearly didn't have. I apologised for inconveniencing them both made my excuses and left. That was the last debt collecting job I ever did.

Keep it in the family.

The alcohol industry isn't the only one trying to take money. It also works the other way.

In a part of town that was described as up and coming lies this large sports bar. It was situated at the top of a long straight road and the redevelopment of the area had brought with it the younger posh urbanites. These young professionals were property owners and demanded quality. The problem was that the majority of the area was still lived in by the local working-class community who had their own way of doing things. So, a sort of two tier system fell into place where the two social groups manage to co-exist in close proximity without ever really interacting. Except for in our sports bar, here the different classes mingled for big sporting events, football games and Saturday night debauchery.

A group of locals were congregated around one of the tables, we knew the group and although they were a dodgy bunch we were all on nodding terms and they had never given me any trouble. One of the lads in the group had warrants outstanding so was on the run, another was there with his missus. Her arm was in plaster where it had been broken a few weeks before. Her and her fella had got into a drunken argument and he had run her over. This was not uncommon, and both had been arrested multiple times for domestic violence against each other. Another one of the lads in the group was a local dealer, thief, and con-artist. Today his dad was with him and between the group the drinks were flowing freely, and everyone was in a party mood. Round after round of drinks were ordered at the bar by the group but it was only ever the dad who came up to pay. His son would loudly offer to get the round in while waving a wad of notes in the air which he would then give to his dad who would get up and go to the bar.

At the end of a very busy day the tills where emptied and tallied up. It was found that a large proportion of the £20 notes were counterfeit. Nearly £200 in total had been taken by the staff through the day. The cameras were checked, and a pattern started to emerge, every time the dad came up, he paid with a £20 note but would only buy two to three drinks maximum every time. As the fake notes were counted they tallied exactly with the number of visits he made to the bar. The son had brought a few thousand worth of forged notes for a percentage of what they cost and was trying to pass them on wherever he could. When it went to court it turned out that the father allegedly knew nothing about it, he was just being used by the son to handle the cash, so the son could avoid getting caught.

Stay awake and hallucinate.

Let's be real about this, we are in it for the money. We all have bills to pay and the wolves are snapping at our heels increasingly these days. So, when the opportunity comes up to make a few quid pretty quickly, you take it. Festival season is for us a glut of work which lasts for a few months through the summer and people can make a decent amount of cash. As usual the phone had gone off and the offer of work had come through. This time it was working a rather large Uk festival manning the gates. It was an interesting weekend for a number of reasons, not least of all because that weekend I worked a 50 hour straight shift with limited breaks.

How the festival scene works is that a security company will be contracted in for either the entire thing or various parts of the festival. That company will then hire staff for the event. Normally a company will have regular people on the books and a list of ad-hoc staff. Once they have exhausted that list the work gets sub-contracted out, this process can happen several times. What this does is dilute the professionalism of the staff and create a situation where colleges may be working side by side but are receiving a different hourly rate. It also means that the chain of command becomes blurred and the reliability of teammates becomes questionable. It is not unusual to have people not turn up or turn up and realise its hard work so quit. Or quit because they are on a gate somewhere when the y assumed they would be working as Beyonce's personal bodyguard. The list goes on, but what this means for people like me is that there are a lot of hours on offer and since you can barely sleep at a festival anyway you may as well make some money.

For me this was a new company that I had done some bits for so was still trying to make a name for myself. Unfortunately this often means accepting the shitty end of the stick for a while. For me the entire festival was like this. Firstly, it rained constantly. Not a little bit, but to biblical proportions. Entrances were closed and the local farmers were making a killing dragging vehicles out of the mud. The fields turned into a swamp and your feet would sink out of view into the ooze that was a mixture of mud and overflowed sceptic tanks with every step. Staff were dropping like flies and management were struggling to plug the gaps.

My first post was on a gated campsite entrance, here people had brought weekend camping tickets and the field was littered with everything thing from converted builder's vans and buses to top of the range American style motorhomes that cost more than most peoples houses. I was partnered with an African guy I had not met before. He was tall and skinny and spoke barely any English. To start with any questions the festivalgoers asked him where met with a shrug and a finger point towards me. Then after an hour or two he started to disappear for longer and longer periods until eventually he stopped returning altogether. I had stopped worrying about it as he was no help anyway until a middle-aged woman approached me. She had just come back from watching one of those political singers perform on stage to find her patio furniture missing. She was a little annoyed and wanted to know what security was going to do about it. I hadn't seen my college for over an hour by this stage and was not supposed to leave the gate unattended, so this left me in a bit of a pickle. I explained to the lady that I would do what I can and set off to find my missing partner and get him to man the gate while I searched for the chairs. It didn't take long to find him. And unfortunately, I had also found the chairs. As it had been raining solidly he had found some tarp and slung it between two vehicles making a nice little tent. He was underneath this in the dry. He was sat in one of the ladies' chairs and he had his legs crossed at the ankles resting on the other one. He seemed very cosy until I started yelling at him. Returning the chairs to the women I had to say that I found them but could not say where.

The day wore on and the shift change had come and gone. The security was on a twelve-hour rotation and we were now well into the night. I was now posted to a different gate. This time I was alone with only the radio for company. I would listen to the chatter going on inside the festival and the occasional staff call out for a comfort break. That's the correct term for needing the loo. I was glad things had settled as it had been a busy few hours, the gate I was on was closed due to the awful weather conditions but still people were trying to get in this way. I had had many heated conversations with disgruntled festival goers who could see their campsite from the gate but told they would have to go around. It had been a tough few hours and the rain was still coming down. My poncho and waterproofs were helping but by now everything was soggy and as the sun had gone down the cold had started to find its way into the gaps. I had taken to pacing up and down to stay awake, this was a trick I used often, and I used to imagine the French convict Papillion in his cell pacing from one wall to the other, night after night, year after year. While doing this I would listen to the distant chatter of the festival, I could see the stage lights over the horizon and the radio kept me informed. They had taken a first aid casualty out on a pallet using some kind of forklift as the ambulance couldn't access the main site. There were reports of organised thefts from the campsites and the group had been spotted and were being chased across the grounds. All posts were told to stay vigilant. Fifteen minutes or so went by and a set of blazing headlamps on full beam were racing towards me. I stepped out into the entranceway only to jump back to the side. The large 4x4 type vehicle was not stopping and crashed through the gate and sped off down the lane. I radioed it through and listened as the chase continued. There was no way I could have stopped it and it was the most exciting point of my weekend.

It's the last day and I am still going. Apart from a few stops to eat I have been on shift the entire time. My vision is going blurry and at times I feel dizzy. It's an odd feeling but just a few more hours. Today is the toughest of all, the weather has been awful with the rain continuing to fall. Vehicles have been abandoned and families with crying children are traipsing through the mud like some kind of disaster movie. The last day for everyone has become an exercise in getting through. The only happy people were the farmers who were appearing in numbers. They had started charging £40-50 to tow the cars out of the fields and into the roads. Some had tried by themselves and either got stuck with the wheels spinning chucking up mud or slid off into other parked vehicles. We were trying to liaise with them as best as possible as we needed their help. While all this was happening, some people were acting very selfishly and blocking the road off by just abandoning their cars on the roadside to go off to collect their stuff on foot. This created major problems as the tractors couldn't get past. It eventually reached a tipping point where some of the abandoned cars had to be moved or nothing would be going anywhere.

One of the cars belonged to a lady I had spoken to. She got out of her car and when I had explained that she was blocking the tractors she said she would be ten minutes and then be back. Her manner was confrontational and unpleasant however we had been asked to be as accommodating as possible so off she went. Eventually we reached the point where something had to be done so the farmers hooked up the chains to the abandoned cars and dragged the thirty yards down the road. Once this was done the evacuation could continue and slowly but surely families and their possessions were dragged out of the mud onto the hard road where they could then start the journey home. It was exhausting work and I was really not in the mood when the abandoned car lady returned demanding to know where her car was. Over three hours had passed, and I angrily told her it was down there as I pointed in the general direction. She was not at all happy with this and told me she was a police officer and would have me charged with TWOC'ing. I had to ask somebody what that was, and it turns out it means taking without consent. In other words, she was accusing me of stealing her car. She swore and threatened and made a massive scene like a two-year-old having a temper tantrum. I tried to stay calm and explained if she had not left it to cause the obstruction or returned in the time she said she would this would not have happened. But as always in cases like this she would accept no responsibility for the situation and demanded to take my number. Angrily she tried to gather support from the surrounding people but by then no-one cared. She did complain to the company, but no further action was taken. All that was left to do was take the few hours drive home and I could get so much needed sleep.

Over the years I have worked with many companies, some have been good, some have been bad, and some have been so awful as to make their actions criminal. There are two that I have worked with that stand out for the right reasons. The first was Evolution show services run by a guy called Steve. Every time we went to a job run by these guys Steve and his lovely wife would go above and beyond for the needs of the staff. The second is Tom and Armasec Security ltd. I worked with these guys for quite a few years and I have always found them fair and a pleasure to deal with. Unfortunately, Evolution stopped working in the security field but Armasec go from strength to strength and if I ever renewed my license Tom would be the first person I would call for work.

For the purposes of full disclosure, I still work with both of these gents in various ways and consider them friends, but I am not plugging them in anyway. I am just stating that a good company is hard to find, so if you are lucky enough to find one. Show them loyalty.

5: Drugs

When we look at drugs the market is huge, a lot of people want a little something extra for there big Saturday night. And there is no shortage of people to feed that need. From the lowest level guy dabbling a bit and selling a few wraps to his mates right through to the large incredibly well organised, well financed and very violent gangs.

What a lot of people don't realise is that a lot of event and venue owners know they need a certain amount of drugs to make the night a success. Can you imagine a festival, any festival with a zero tolerance on drugs? They realise that for many, drugs are a large part of the experience and if the punters aren't getting the party they want then they go somewhere else. It really is that simple. Yes, in public they will all stand there po- faced spouting the party line of zero tolerance but in the dressing room the artists will have a blind eye turned to certain practises and the punters get to party hard with the recreational drug of choice.

Before we delve into this world I just want to address the elephant in the room.

Now I am not saying right or wrong I am just stating the reality of the situation.

If you work in a bar or club in any capacity, if you are involved in facilitating people's ability to drink alcohol then you are helping to supply the worst drug out there. Alcohol kills more people than all the illegal drugs combined. Fact!

It's not just the punters.

Jason was one of the doormen in our company. He was also a bodybuilder. Now in my experience I find there are variants in types of people that do this. Some are really nice people that just want to look good, others are complete egotistical twats that have the mis-informed opinion that because they have big arms they can feel superior to everyone. Jason fell heavily into the latter category. Now for the sake of the story I will give my opinion on the subject. While I admire and respect anyone that dedicates themselves in the pursuit of excellence whatever the field, for me bodybuilding is a tough one to understand. You have guys and girls that want to grow to excessive proportions, where their frame was only designed to support 14 stone they have buffed up to 20. All bodybuilders are at there weakest when they look there best. It is an unhealthy practise and quite often points to some underlying issues.

Body dysmorphia is a mental illness. It effects different people in different ways. An anorexic will look at their reflection and see a disgusting fat blob no matter how emaciated they are, some bodybuilders see there reflection as skinny and weedy no matter how much mass they pack on. So, like a lot of guys to cover his own insecurities Jason turned to the weights where he met others like him and together they convinced themselves that big is bad. The amount of times I have seen gym bunnies like this go to a martial arts gym and watch as their sugar pedestal melts before your very eyes as they quickly realise they have no actual fighting skills. I don't include everyone in this by the way as you get guys that train for functional strength that are ripped and let's be honest if the worlds strongest man kicked off in your bar you are going to have problems. These people train for ability not vanity and it's the difference between having a Ferrari car with a mini engine or a mini car with a Ferrari engine. So, Jason fell headlong into the scene, first it was a few protein shakes, then a few enhancers and a bit of Creatine until soon he was sticking needles in his arse and was convinced of his own superiority. Steroid abuse is widespread and pretty mainstream in certain sections of our community and James saw a profit to be made.

He liked to wear clothes that little bit to tight and expose as much of his chest as possible, he would chew gum continuously and sneer at anybody walking by. His attitude sucked and because of all these reasons people didn't take to him very well and he would often get punched. Some would argue that being huge for a doorman is an asset, in this case it was the polar opposite. Because he had no people skills he couldn't talk a situation down and because he was hugely disproportionate in body shape due to the weights and the steroids he couldn't fight either. In fact, its why he got punched so often as he couldn't get his arms up in time. In fact, people like this are a complete liability and let's not even start on the famed roid-rage. What's odd is that I have worked with some competitive bodybuilders over the years and they were really nice people who were good at the job, it's just that for some reason you get these guys every so often.

It turns out that running the door of a busy club can be beneficial if your side line is flogging steroids. Other doormen from across the town would pop by on there way to and from shift to say hi and collect their purchases. He had a good little thing going. Eventually he had been in one too many unnecessary fights and the rumours of his dealing got too much to ignore and the company quietly let him go. For me I always try to avoid these sorts of people as they will get you hurt.

Ketamine coma.

Drugs go in and out of fashion just like clothes or music genres and as the years go by the tastes for what the people want their drugs to do for them changes. In fact, you could even argue that to listen to the monotonous thud thud of modern music you need to be on some sort of chemical enhancement. But I'm guessing that's just me getting old, I've always preferred a tune and lyrics. If we go back to the 60's hallucinogens and Marijuana were the drugs of choice. The music genres of the day lent themselves to this and songs like White rabbit were born. The music would take you on a journey and we all know the old LP covers made great tables for building spliffs on.

Some drugs bring you up and some drugs bring you down and knowing which is which can really change your experience. Hallucinogenics, acid, LSD, these have mostly died out in the modern club scene. Try doing a Jungle night on magic mushrooms and you will see why. Weed is still very popular for concerts and festivals, not so much clubs. Modern day weed is more of an after-party drug. A way to come down from the amphetamines and Coke. What you will find these days is that Coke is rife, club toilets after a busy Saturday night are littered with little see through ziplock bags and scrunched up wraps like confetti after a wedding.

Coke makes people feel good!!!! Yes, I know it's bad but why is it so popular? It gives people confidence, energy, and in some cases a personality and when someone tries a little friendly snort with there mate in the toilet it's hard to go back to just booze. With club nights going till 6am these days a solid 10 hours of drinking isn't going to work so how else are they going to stay awake? It also takes away fear and can make you feel invincible. This is also the reason a lot of bouncers in the old days used it. It got them through a long shift, now we are fuelled by multiple cans of Red Bull (other options are available). The down side of this is that some 18-year-old, 10 stone student can think he's the incredible hulk. It's not unusual to have someone half your size outside your front door bare-chested arms splayed demanding to fight everyone despite the fact he's never had a fight in his life. But you can't dismiss him as these guys can be very dangerous. They will take actions without thought of consequence, they often feel no pain, and some become incredibly strong. Or maybe it's the guy that you have chucked out for whatever reason and he's got nowhere to go. The drugs are racing through him and he can't sit still so he tries to talk to you for 3 hours bobbing up and down and skipping from foot to foot, gurning and sniffing, every fourth word is innit.

You can't do a festival these days without hearing the little hiss of escaping compressed air coming from the bushes. Pssst! It's like the foliage wants to whisper you a secret. Noz has become incredibly popular and even if you don't go clubbing you are likely to have seen the little metallic grey capsules littering the parks where the youth have been hanging out.

The ease and cheapness of drugs means that it continues to grow in popularity and the clubbers attitude towards drugs in general is acceptance. For a lot of them it is just another part of a normal weekend out.

Its Saturday night around Midnight, the club is busy and as usual the punters are partying hard. All around me are 18-25 year olds trying to binge drink themselves into oblivion. The sign of a good night these days seems to be the less you remember the better it was. Well for this young lady her memory of this night will last a lifetime. I am stood at the door when a young girl comes rushing up. "You have to help me" she says grabbing my arm and trying to pull me into the club. She is obviously distressed, so I follow her to the seating area to the side of the dance floor. There are two girls sat there, both maybe 20, very pretty and wearing very little. One of them is moaning slightly, her head tilted forward leaning across her friend, a line of drool is running down her chin. It is obvious she is under the effects of something. At this point she is conscious so myself and my colleague help her up and take her to the front lobby where the light is better, and we can make a better assessment. Its obvious this girl needs medical attention so my partner rings an ambulance while I try to administer first aid. Some people think our job is easy but here's the thing while I am doing this I am constantly monitoring the situation as I am aware I am vulnerable. Certain people will taker advantage of this situation and may try to attack us when we are not paying attention. Others may try to smuggle contraband into the club or steal. We still must look after everyone else at these times as well.

By this stage the young lady is led in an approximation of the recovery position, her muscles have spasmed and she has gone rigid. Her eyes are wide open and staring but she doesn't seem to be responsive. I ask her friends what had she taken. They told me she has had nothing. Friends often do this in some misguided belief they are protecting their mates. I asked again, this time reinforcing the seriousness of the situation. Finally, one of the girls said she had drunk half a bottle of vodka and taken Ketamine before coming to the club.

This is called pre-loading and is very common. People will drink a large amount of booze very quickly or ingest their drug of choice just before coming to the club so when they arrive the effects have yet to kick in and they look fine to us. That is exactly what this girl had done. As a late night club we had only been open an hour. She had come in as a ticking time bomb just waiting to explode.

The ambulance was on its way, but it had already been 20 mins and the girl is still comatose. Her breathing is regular but shallow and she was making this funny low moan. A small pool of spit had formed around her face as her eyes stared forward. Finally, the ambulance arrived and with a flurry of activity they set to work. This was not the first time they had seen this, and they knew exactly what to do. We as the security team went back to running the club and just put it to the back of our mind.

Two weeks later I arrived for work and was putting the barriers out for the smoking area when a car pulled up. The passenger door opened and the girl who had collapsed got out. She was crying as she thanked me for our kindness and for looking after her. I said it was nothing. Her reply was shocking. She explained how she was completely conscious the whole time, she could hear every word and see every action. Her body wouldn't let her speak or move but she was aware of everything that happened that night.

I'll fight a drug dealer for £10.

I had landed myself a job in a casino. It was regular work and for the most part even though it is the biggest casino in the South-west major trouble was rare. We would work in different team numbers depending on the day. Monday through Thursday we only had two members of the security team on. Friday and Saturdays, we would move to four. Sunday, we had three, the biggest gambling day of the week as that's when the players come out. The serious people don't want the game ruined by some drunken stag throwing £10 down on a Saturday night. The security team itself was quite small and had some really good guys on it over time. Unfortunately, the guy in charge was not one.

Have you heard the term jacket-filler? This means someone whose only use is to make up numbers. But he was worse than that. He was a coward and a manipulator, hated and despised by the team, the casino staff, and punters alike. He stood about 5"10 with a chunky bordering on fat frame that he tried to keep in check with weights and would turn up for every shift with his protein shake just in case someone didn't notice his guns. He also had a strangely fat head and was so filled with his own importance he reminded me of Mr Toad from Wind in the Willows.

He once called for back-up because a guy was wearing a tap out t-shirt so must be an MMA fighter.

You get the picture. I wasn't keen on this guy and spent the entire time I worked there defending him from angry putters who he had riled up. He would never be physical himself and would hide behind the other guys every time. This is where the problem started. In the casino tonight was a mid-level drug dealer. Casinos have a lot of criminals in them, it's a place they can do business and mingle with there peers. One of the top Triad bosses was a regular. Normally these guys give us no trouble, they have far bigger fish to fry. But like the c-list celebrities and lower league football players the lower end of the pecking order sometimes come with a large chip on there shoulder. The drug dealer/criminal in question was acting like an idiot. Drunk and verbally abusive he had become threatening and needed to leave. I was called to the gaming floor to see my mate blockhead trying to calm him down. The more he tried to appease him the more he fanned the flames of the bully. The dealer could see the fear in him and was disregarding him completely. He had threatened him and pushed him with no consequence so now had his measure. Blockhead knew who he was and was afraid of him. I didn't know who he was and as I grabbed him and dragged him backwards towards the doors he told me several times. By the time I threw his angry arse into the street I knew exactly who he was. He had informed me he ran a criminal gang and was a drug dealer known for some pretty heavy violence and was going to fuck me up in several ways. He was very vocal in his dislike of me and was pretty pissed that I had apparently disrespected him like that. He told me he was going to burn my house down with my kids in it and get some crackheads to rape my missus and stab me up. Unfortunately, he had done time for similar offences and its whispered he'd got away with a lot more, so these weren't just idle threats.

Then the intimidation started. The problem with working a door is that the bad guys know exactly where you are going to be. Firstly, he and his cronies would do slow drive-by's in blacked out range rovers, windows cranked open just enough, so we could see the staring eyes within as a trail of weed smoke drifted out. Then people would start to walk by, pulling aside their jacket to reveal a knife or just holding one in their hand as they walked past. This carried on for a few weeks topped up with verbal threats and phone calls. I spent that time nervous and on edge, every night on shift felt like a week, my appetite had all but disappeared and I was snapping at everybody. Living like this was getting on top of me and my nerves were shot. It needed to end. I made some phone calls of my own to get it sorted. I let the right people know what was happening and that I wanted to square it away. I offered to meet this guy and get it sorted, I was tired of the games and wanted it over.

As it happened the situation reached the ears of one of his bosses through a mutual friend and as he did not want to muddy the waters or bring attention to himself or his operations he spoke to the drug dealer and reigned him in. And just like that it stopped. Sometimes you need to ask yourself, is it worth it?

Buried treasure.

I was asked to work covert security at one of the biggest music festivals in Europe. Occasionally it takes a year off but mostly once a year an entire town with all the infrastructure pops up for a few days in the middle of the countryside. The whole process to set up and take down takes months but the festival itself is less than a week.

We had been tasked to be covert security teams. Our role was to monitor the festival goers by blending in with the punters. That was hard as I was partnered with an ex-sergeant who did the full 20+ years and farted constantly. He was so obviously military that he stood out like a sore thumb. It doesn't matter what you dress these guys in there bearing and constant use of the word outstanding gives them away. For four days I followed behind this guy as we yomped from stage to stage and did endless laps of the carpark. He liked a good march and just couldn't adapt to the pace of the festival goers. The farting just made it worse. He would just let them go wherever he was with no apparent concern or embarrassment. I struggled to stay upwind of him the entire time.

It was here I learned just how ingenious the dealers could be. Five months before a few hikers had walked across the countryside. Dressed as ramblers with their cagoules and gaters they clambered over gates and wandered through the fields. It all looked innocent enough until you learnt that in the rucksacks they were carrying were large quantities of drugs bagged up in watertight wrapping which they were burying as they went. The co-ordinates of the stashes were noted and then it was just a waiting game.

Time went past, and the festival began to sprout up. The stages were built, compost toilets installed and all the power, roadworks, fences, and everything else required was erected and built in the next few months. A small city had been built behind mile after mile of fencing. As the years have gone on the security measures have become increasingly robust and checks and searches applied at every gate. But unknown to the organisers they had built the fencing with the buried stashes on the inside of the walls.

Our ramblers were back, they had brought early bird tickets and were now dressed the same as the other festival goers. As the queue slowly snaked towards the search tables the pair kicked their bags forward a few inches every time it moved forward. When they finally got to the search areas they put their bags and tents on the table for the security to check and made small talk with the guys. They had no reason to be nervous as they had nothing suspicious on them. Apart from the GPS that is. But in amongst all the other things and with a long queue of people behind the guys saw no reason to question it. The ramblers made it through the gates and with the rest of the punters made there way into the festival. They got set up, and went and found a beer tent. That's where they sat for a few hours while they waited for darkness to fall. When it did they went on their version of a treasure hunt and dug up the packages buried all those months ago.

Vomit display.

I have no idea what this girl was on, but she was out there with Pluto as they say. We were at a high end corporate function. Christmas was coming, and the month of December is filled with office workers and middle management trying to hold their booze and get off with the pretty PA. The venue we are in is one of Brunel's best structures. Tonight, it has been made out into a winter wonderland and hired out for office parties. Most of the time these are great fun to do but they have their own rules. You cannot treat the guests the same way as you would the customers in a bar. A lot of these people have spent a lot of money on the tickets and once the sit-down meal has ended the band will start. People who don't normally drink will binge to celebrate the birth of Christ, office workers and phone operators will get a bit edgy with there mates and scurry off for the occasional sniff in the toilets. All the while the office undercurrent will run through while everyone tries to drunkenly snog everyone else. When the band stops, and the lights go up it is our job to clear the building. Different venues have different ways of achieving this from the local bar where the landlord gives the punters a countdown before he lets his two large aggressive German Shepard's out to the large nightclub that forms a human wall with it's security team and herds the punters out the door like sheep. We had to be a little more diplomatic here, and the job of clearing the room was often a long drawn out process. You would have time at the bar and allow a drinking up period, but still people would stand there chatting holding a nearly full drink and making no effort to drink it. You would politely ask them and do a lap to allow them some time. You sometimes had to do this several times. It always amazed me how the wealthy middle-class professionals could be so rude. The majority of our guests were very nice people but there was always a small percentage.

A young lady sat at the table alone. The tables sat ten and were circular in shape covered with a large tablecloth. Strewn across this was the detritus of the nights partying. Empty bottles and half empty glasses lay amongst the party poppers and disposable cameras, directly in front of the young lady was an empty cocktail glass. I had asked her to start to make her way out five minutes ago, this had fallen on deaf ears as she was still sat there. I went and spoke to her again noting her pupils were dilated and her speech slurred. I left her sat there and went to speak to a manager to see if we could locate any of her friends. Almost everyone had gone by this time and the waiting staff were moving round the tables like ants collecting up the rubbish and starting to reset everything, so we could do it all again tomorrow.

I went back to the young lady and asked her name, her skin looked clammy and pale and she did not look well. Suddenly her shoulders hunched forward, and her mouth opened to release a stream of vomit that erupted out of her like a scene from the Exorcist, which then hit the base of the cocktail glass and ricocheted back out to hit her square in the face. Nobody likes other peoples vomit so I took a big step back as she looked up at me. Vomit chunks were stuck in her hair and the liquid ran down her face. The front of her top was covered in puke as she sat there and started to sob.

6: The good, bad old days

When I started on the doors it was back in the days before the SIA, back before CCTV and human rights. Back then people got slapped and that was the end of it. You were chosen for your qualities and the vast majority of bouncers back then were monsters of men who were very skilled at violence. Now you can argue that that is not the way to deal with the problem, but I would ask you this. If I said we are going to play a game of football, you on one team and myself on the other. Your team must obey a very strict set of rules. You cannot do a lot of things and all eyes are watching you in the hope you fuck up. And if you do, the powers that be will come down on you with everything they have. The other team have no rules, they can do whatever they like. They also know that you are hamstrung by the rules and have to obey them. They also know that almost always they will not be penalised for any wrongdoing. Which team do you think will win? Which side would you rather be on? This is the reality of being a bouncer in the modern world. Everyone knows their rights, and no-one has any respect for authority. It gets more dangerous every day as we are asked to deal with seriously violent people with no real training and no toys. If you are a copper at least you get a baton, pepper spray and handcuffs. We run a genuine risk of prison for defending ourselves and the majority of the public think we are violent bullies. This could not be further from the truth. Once maybe, but these days you need to be so much more than that.

Many years ago, at a bar in Yate called Spirals I watched a team of bouncers attack a lone shirtless man as a pack. They surrounded and goaded him. He lashed out when one of the black clad men came into range. The lone warrior was literally half the size of some of these men but refused to back down.

I was eighteen years old and had met this girl who I felt I needed to impress. We had met in a local bar and I had given her the full treatment. Every single move my young self knew had been used and to my surprise and delight she had agreed to a date the following weekend. Now, I could have taken her to the local town and I'm sure that would have been more than enough for her, but no. I had to make some sort of grandiose gesture and try to show off, so I told here we were going clubbing. Now when you live in a small town and that town has no clubs, clubbing is actually harder than you would think. You either go to one of the late-night bars that tries to be a club and pretended you're were having a great time while the local lads fought with the squaddies from the camp down the road over whatever girls were available. O you arranged transport and took a journey. As I was showing off I took the latter and decided to go to Spiral's in Yate. I had been there once before and in my small-town mind the place was huge, and I had felt like a tourist in a foreign land as I gawked at the spectacle around me. I have since moved on and now see Yate for what it is but back then it was a world of wonder and new experiences. So, because I had been there once I thought I can take this girl and impress her knickers off with my cosmopolitan ways and knowledge of city clubs. I had hired a taxi at no small expense as back then I didn't drive, and I made sure I did the whole opening the door for her scene when we pulled up outside her house. She climbed into the taxi and we were off. The driver must have thought I was a complete dick as I chattered away and told her about the club and what it was like, desperately trying to fill the space with noise so we didn't have to sit there in silence. Eventually we made it to Yate and the cab driver pulled up, again I rushed around the back of the car to open the door and held out my hand for her to take as she got out. I was trying so hard to be a gentleman, so I took her arm and we walked towards the club. Now if my memory serves me right as its been a very long time since I've been there, the club is accessed by a pedestrianised bit and as we rounded the corner we could see a large group.

What I could see was a group of about eight very large guys with huge backs and shovel-like hands. They were all wearing black trousers and white shirts and had formed a circle around this guy. The guy in the middle was maybe ten stone, skinny and quite pale. He was bare chested and had his shirt in in hand. He was using this to keep the bouncers at bay. They would get a little to close and he would lash out forcing the bigger men back. The bouncers were goading him on, daring him to take a shot. They were talking amongst themselves while they were doing this, making jokes at this guys expense. The guy in the middle was outmanned and out gunned, but he wasn't going to go down without a fight and was trying to hold them back by flailing his arms and feet at anyone close enough. Soon the bouncers got bored of this, the cat and mouse game had gone on long enough and they descended on this shirtless guy beating him mercilessly. They knocked him to the floor where they then kicked and stamped him. He tried to rise and at one point made it to his knees only to be forced back down with a crushing knee to the ribs. The bouncers kicked him around for a bit and then made there way back to the entrance to the club. The shirtless guy lay on the floor broken and unconscious. My date and I looked at each other and very gingerly made our way into the club, neither one of us knowing what to say after what we had just witnessed.

Yeah but, no but.

The club was heaving, it was one of the club's busier promotions that offered a night of drum and bass guaranteed to assault your ears. The promotion was run by a few lads in there early 20's and brought a lot of mates with them who would be d'jing. They in turn brought their mates so the club was at capacity with 18-25yr olds with eyes the size of dustbin lids. Drugs are part of the scene and most them were on something a little stronger than a beer. The music was rhythmic with a heavy bassline that reverberated around the club. At the front of the packed dancefloor the giant speakers pulsed in time as the clubbers writhed and gyrated in an almost hypnotic state, heat from the dancing bodies made the air sticky with sweat and the strobe lights cut through the dry ice momentarily blinding anyone who looked directly at them. Packed together they created a sea of bobbing heads that went all the way from the back of the dancefloor to the DJ booth at the front where the DJ hunched over his desk spinning the tunes and guiding the crowd like an urban conductor to an ASBO orchestra.

Right at the front of the dancefloor directly underneath the booth there was an implosion of people and a ripple like a sonic boom swept backwards through the tightly packed crowd as they were pushed back and tried to regain balance. A gap appeared in the sea of heads and people started shouting.

A fight had started.

We started pushing our way through the dancers, shoulder barging them aside to create a pathway. There is no time to say "excuse me "in moments like this. We forced our way through to see a group of lads around twenty years of age all grabbing hold of each other and lashing out. It looked like they were all giving as good as they got so with no obvious aggressor I chose to grab the lad nearest to me. Being very aware of the flailing arms I hooked my guy under one arm and around the neck with the other and started dragging him backwards through the crowd. Scot who had made his way across the dancefloor parallel to me appeared from nowhere and grabbed this other lad who was trying to take a swing at my head. Mike, another ds appeared to join the fray. He was old school, in his early fifties but solid as a rock. A large bald head sat atop a powerful 6-foot frame that was squeezed into his jacket. He decided that he was going to escort his antagonist out the old-fashioned way. As he grabbed his guy, the young man made the mistake of lashing out. Mike grabbed him by the shoulders and engulfed him, pulling him in close with no escape. He then proceeded to walk this guy across the club. With every step he would land a short headbutt into the poor lad's temple. As he was holding him up the lad would stumble but not fall. Bang! The impact of Mikes forehead would send the guy's head snapping back, Bang! On the next step he would do it again. All the way across the dancefloor he butted him while grumbling under his breath. Each of us dragged our respective fighter towards the exit where we converged and threw them into the street where they shouted and threatened but nothing came of it. My guess is Mike's guy had a monstrous headache the next day.

How to be a one-man gang.

I met Matty early on in my career and we became firm friends and partners in crime. Looking like a young Marlon Brando and standing over six feet he was an imposing guy. He was young and started the doors early but had taken to it like a fish to water. We had this trick we used to pull to quieten down the unruly customers but more on that later.

This was a busy nightclub of the day. The dress code was still smart, and we were sporting white shirts and dickie bows. The club was situated in the popular part of town and was built over three floors. Each floor had its own bars and dancefloors, and each would play different flavours of the music of the time. By this stage I had met Matty two or three times and we had worked a few shifts together. Tonight, he was monitoring the bar and I was circling the dancefloor and stairs area. The dry ice was so thick you could taste it and the lights would cut through them in a laser show that looked like an alien spaceship had landed. We had no radios back then and usually glass breaking or a shout from the DJ box would be our first alert to trouble. This was a big club and it took a while to move around the whole area so as I had done the lap and was making my way back I noticed Matty in a heated debate with a group of lads at the bar. They were waving their arms and being very animated. I started to walk over towards them but was on the other side of the dancefloor, so it would take a few seconds. One of the group started prodding Matty in the chest. He fell silent, I know now this means someone is about to get launched but didn't then. Matty looked down at his crisp white shirt, then raised his eyes to look at the guy pointing. With that Matty launched a bomb of a punch. Pointy guy went down like he had been shot. Matty then moved on to the other members of the group and was lashing out at anything in range. One of the group tried to grab Matty from behind and he shot his head back exploding the guys nose. He then spun round grabbed him and threw him bodily into the bar. By this time, I am running through the dancers trying to cover ground and get to the outnumbered Matty. By the time I finally got there he was just finishing off the last of his opponents. Around him lay what was left of the group, two of the guys had ran, two more lay unconscious with a third softly moaning and cradling what looked like a broken arm. Together we started to drag them towards the fire escape. I was amazed by this display of prowess and asked him what martial arts did he study. He laughed and said "none"." How the hell did you learn to fight like that?" I asked. His reply was pretty straight forward. "I come from Knowle west" he said, "when you got presents on Christmas day if you wanted to still have them by boxing day, you had to fight for them". Basically, he grew up doing for real what I had up to now only been practising in the safety of my classes. We became tight after that and had quite a few difficult nights over the years. It was always reassuring to have a one-man gang around.

When old school is still required.

Sometimes the training you receive for the SIA license and the type of person the current laws attract don't really cut the mustard. The seriously violent, the criminals and nutcases. The genuinely hard men and psychopaths. These people have been slowly driven out of the industry. Yes, some refuse to go quietly and become security consultants while other turn into eighteen stone overpaid glass collectors but in the main they are a dying breed within the modern-day security industry.

Myself and Matty had had a call about taking on a pub. It was a pretty rough place in a bad part of town where gangs and drugs are rampant. The whole area of the city is deprived, and crime is through the roof. Not far away is one of Britain's most dangerous streets where shootings and stabbing are an almost weekly occurrence. The landlord wanted us to go and have a chat regards taking over the security on a Friday and Saturday night. We met him at the door and he ushered us into the office where he sent one of the barmaids off with our coffee order. He explained that he was looking for a new team to run the door as the last lot were not up to the job and he claims to have sacked them. Some of what he was saying was very vague and didn't seem to ring true. We decided that before we reached any decisions we would go and take a better look. Given the area and clientele we knew it was not going to be an easy venue and we wanted to know what we were taking on.

We had come back and had settled in the bar with a pint, already you could feel the malicious stares of the locals. This did not have a friendly feel to it and being honest we weren't surprised as a lot of local inner-city pubs are just like this, especially in the daytime. We managed to get chatting to an old black chap. He had gaps in his teeth and a scar that ran across his chin. He was happy to talk and after a few minutes of pleasantries we started to ask a few more probing questions. We wanted to know what had become of the last team and was it the way the landlord had described it.

With a guffaw that turned into a series of hacking coughs the old boy told the tale of what happened. The previous team had been brought in and they had been handpicked apparently by the security company. These guys were going to clean up Dodge and put a stop to the drugs and violence. They did well initially and threw out a few of the lower end dealers, even managed to bully a few of the local scrotes into not causing trouble there anymore. Until one day it started effecting profits. Now the local criminal gangs run the drugs and they do that with very serious violence and the only thing these people understand and respect is greater violence. You can dress it up however you like but these people are very real, and they are out there.

One Saturday night the boys arrived for there shift and as the walked towards the club they were surrounded by a group of guys. They were then marched round the car-park to the back of the pub where they were ordered to kneel. Some of the men were brandishing machetes and they stood over them menacingly waving the blades in the air. Two of the guys each pulled a sawn-off shotgun out from under their coats and placed them in the mouths of the bouncers. They then quietly explained that they were fucking up business and were going to get themselves shot if they didn't pack it in. The gang explained to them how it was going to be while they both nodded furiously unable to answer with mouths full of gun barrel.

The old boy that told us this then explained that the footage of the entire incident had oddly disappeared as had the bouncers. They were never seen at that venue again. We declined to take the job which I think you can understand. A couple of white boys like us would have ended with a similar fate I am sure.

7: Violence

Football fans.

I hadn't been working long. I'm not sure of the year or game as I am not a football fan so don't follow it, but it was the Euro's I think. The one where Beckham did something he shouldn't.

I had turned up for work to find the bar absolutely rammed full of people. We had three members of security on that day. The venue itself was a busy centre of town pub where you had to go down a few steps to go into the main bar. It had two entrances on either side of the building both leading out into busy city streets. We would normally have one on either door and a floater that monitored the inside and helped man the door when required. When we arrived for our shift the bar was already full of people anticipating the game. As always, the mood is excitable, and the beer is flowing freely. Gangs of mate's crowd around there chosen tables discussing possible outcomes and taking the piss out of each other. When it comes to football this is the best bit where everyone is jovial, and a party atmosphere prevails. Although sometimes it doesn't last. Did you know that during the world cup domestic violence rockets by over a third? Disappointed by their chosen teams performance they lash out at family members and loved ones. I don't get it myself but there is no denying the passion football arouses in people.

Today my job was to be the floater, I was to monitor the crowd without antagonising them and to try to stop any problems before they happened. The bar had a large projector like screen that was showing the game. The usual yelling and jeering was going on as people shouted at the tv telling the players what they should be doing.

Suddenly there was a crash as a pint glass hit the screen and exploded in a shower of glass. Beckham had done whatever it was he did, and the bar was not HP. The pub was standing room only and everyone was elbow to elbow in a sea of replica England tops. I had no idea who had thrown the glass but that paled into insignificance as a stool was flung at the screen. As if on cue everyone started fighting. Even the people who weren't fighting were fighting as they fought to protect their loved ones or just to get clear of the melee. Groups of males were swinging wildly, people were being hit with glasses and chairs. It had become an all-out mass brawl. The first one I had ever seen. In that situation there really wasn't much we could do as the entire pub was fighting so we gathered up the bar staff and pushed them all into the kitchen area where we phoned the police and watched the brawl continue through the kitchen doors portal window.

This is where I learnt of a strategy allegedly used by the police. Now I am not going to say they do this on purpose but over the years the timing of their arrival was too perfect to be coincidence. We phoned them and waited, and waited and then waited some more. By now the combatants were starting to lose the taste for the violence and had slowed down dramatically. Some had even dusted themselves off and shuffled out into the streets like the walking wounded from a zombie movie. This is the exact point the Police rushed in en-masse. Just in time to arrest a few stragglers with no real risk to themselves. I sometimes think back on that day and think could I have done more? The answer I come up with is no. All these years later and I would still do the same thing. When the whole bar erupts and over a hundred people are fighting there really isn't a lot anyone can do until they run out of steam. The Police taught me that.

Nothing like a drive-in movie.

Speaking of gang fights, this is a story told to me by a colleague who was working shop security. He showed me the phone footage he had taken of the event and it was a scary watch. What is even more peculiar is that it was never reported in the mainstream news or papers.

John and I worked together frequently on the club doors of a weekend. In the days John made his money by working as a security guard in a shopping arcade. This was one of those places where a big industrial estate had turned into a shopping centre. It had a lot of the big-name shops and a cinema complex plus a McDonalds drive through, but the good old US of A this was not. Running parallel to the buildings was row after row of parking where families would leave their cars to watch the latest blockbuster movie or buy the latest must have item. Parents were walking around with children being held by the hand while toddlers were taxied around in pushchairs. This was a normal afternoon, a little overcast and grey with a cold breeze that found the gaps in your coat but no rain so far. John had spent many days just like this one doing this so was just trying to get through the shift. It didn't help that he knew he would have another six-hour door shift later after his ten-hour shift today and his feet were already giving him grief.

Then to Johns complete amazement a large group of men that looked to be Eastern European began swarming through the cars. He reckons they numbered around forty. They were armed with hammers, bats, and machetes. At the other end of the carpark another large group appeared with similar numbers. They were also armed with makeshift weapons. They began to charge at one another as families and shoppers fled in terror. Parents were scooping up children as men wielding weapons rushed past to violently clash in the middle of the car park. This is where John starting filming and on the small screen he held up I watched in horrified fascination as the bloodbath unfolded. Women were screaming and dragging kids along. Shoppers who were trapped in their cars were hurriedly trying to reverse away from the violence. At its centre men were bludgeoning each other. One had fallen to the floor and a group of four or five were taking turns stamping on his head. Another man ran over and clubbed one of the group across the back of the head with what looked like a piece of scaffold pole. All around were pockets of men fighting amongst the parked cars, alarms were going off and the phones microphone had picked up the screams of terror.

Then as suddenly as it had started, it stopped. As if there was some pre-arranged signal everyone stopped fighting and ran off in separate directions. Some were dragging fallen comrades so were slower to leave but within five minutes of it starting they had all but disappeared. I don't know why but this never made the local papers. What might scare a lot of middle England is the truth that most of the violence we witness is neither reported or acted upon.

The London firm.

I had just received a phone call. Jumping up I raced around the room looking for my coat, shoes and a little something just in case. That was the proverbial bat phone and when it asked you answered.

One of our guys Steve had just rang, he and his team had had a run-in the night before with a few lads. These lads were big and rowdy and after knocking a lad unconscious they were dragged out of the club by the door team. Threats were made and as they pointed and threatened at the front of the club the usual "we will be back" and "you're going to have it" was yelled menacingly at the guys. This is not unusual and whilst working at a busy club you hear it at least once a week. Only rarely does it come true.

Steve had received a tip off that the lads from last night were part of a well-known door firm from London and that they had a van load of lumps and were driving back down tonight to dish out what they called revenge. Normally we don't take too much notice of this sort of thing but in this instance the threat seemed credible and the source was reliable. So, I found myself rushing around getting ready to drive down to the club for what could be a war.

I got to the club and met the guys, a few of us had come down to support. I was the smallest at seventeen stone and 6'2 and the four of us went inside and took a seat. We tried to blend in with the punters and look inconspicuous, but it wasn't working. The idea was we were just going to hang around, we didn't want to freak out the customers or owners by all hovering around the door as that seemed like overkill. We made sure we were close to the main doors and sipped our cokes while we waited.

Now for those of you that don't know about adrenaline let me tell you it's a bugger at times like these. Time distortion kicks in and minutes feel like hours. It was harder for the door team as they had to carry on as normal while their adrenaline spiked every time a van came around the corner. They would all momentarily freeze and stare as it went by just in case that was the one. They knew that if they came they would come quick and it would be brutal. Every time a van approached they would visualise it screeching to a halt, the doors flying open and a load of tooled up lumps bursting out. We were feeling it too, but as always you can't admit it, so we ripped the piss out of each other and talked about the various customers as they walked past us to kill time.

The shift ended, and nothing happened. The same as 99% of these claims, nothing came of it. The night ended, we all breathed a sigh of relief and went home. But it wasn't a wasted night because we were there for each other and were prepared to back each other up. Had I ignored that phone call then maybe when I needed help I would be ignored.

The grab and drag principal.

What do you do when you have a door team of six and at least double that many are fighting on your dance floor?

It was a busy Saturday night, I was head doorman and had a team of five under me. The venue was a prestigious club on the main strip of town. Its preferred clientele was z, listers local footballers and women with so much fake tan they looked like a Victorian cabinet. The manager was rumoured to use the club to sell coke and had a good little business going on when the V.I.P tables were throwing £600 bottles of Champagne down their neck like it was going out of fashion. The venue had a long bar and through some doors opened out onto a dancefloor. The floor lit up and would pulsate with different colours to the beat of the dance tunes. This was a place to be seen and the wannabees would be out in their finery showing off their wealth and self-importance to each other like Peacocks displaying their tails. All this ego leads to problems and it was not unusual to have to deal with fights from the rival groups and tonight was no exception.

I have no idea what started it. I was on the door at my usual spot monitoring the queues waiting to get in when the radio comes to life. Fight on the dance floor is yelled through my earpiece. I make out panic in the voice. Myself and my colleagues rush towards the dancefloor trying not to knock customers over as we push through the crowd. As always, we are racing to the unknown so will have to make some snap decisions when we get there. There is a large group of men fighting on the dancefloor, some are on the ground, some stood up trading punches. At least one is swinging a Champagne bottle. At first glance two girls also seem to be involved. One is holding her nose as blood streams between her fingers the other has latched on to this guy's hair and is repeatedly slapping the top of his head while another lad punches him as well. The other punters had moved away creating a ring for the opposing parties to fight in.

So, this is a grab and drag. I grabbed the nearest fighter to me and dragged him through the club, on reaching the front I threw him into the street and ran back towards the fight to grab another. My colleagues were doing similar but because we were outnumbered as we were throwing them out they would just run back in behind us to continue fighting. One of the lads was taking a pounding, he was on the floor with this other guy sat astride him reigning down unanswered blows in a great display of ground and pound. He was taking a right beating, so he was my next target. I ran behind the guy on top reached over his head and hooked his nostrils with my fingers dragging his head back. I locked in a choke and ran him through the bar. The skin of his nose had ripped where I had pulled so hard and as I threw him out in the drizzle the rain mixed with the blood making it look far worse. We managed to get most of the groups out of the club where they continued to fight in the street.

Finally, the Police arrived and between us we rounded up all the fighters. The guy with the split nose tried to get me arrested but after viewing the footage it was obvious I had done what I needed to do so no charges were pressed.

I wish I had paid more attention in Wing Chun class.

I had just received a call over the radio from the gaming floor. I had been asked to meet my colleague by the lifts. Waiting for me were two big units. Both guys were over six foot and muscular. They were off duty bouncers from another club and had been playing up a little. As our bar stayed open till five and the casino itself is twenty fours hours every day except Christmas day we often had bouncers and staff come from other venues when their shift had ended. Quite often the guys would use the free parking facility and only stay long enough to get their ticket validated. Others would hang around and de-pressurise from a night of dealing with drunk and aggressive punters. Some would have a drink or two while others would take a turn at the tables. Some would use as a place to meet the girl they had chatted up earlier and they would sit in one of the little corner seats laying it on thick and trying to get lucky.

This particular pair were just being a pain in the arse, annoying the gamblers and trying to chat up women that obviously had partners. It was time for them to leave so they had been politely asked and escorted to the lifts which is where I met them. In the casino the only public entry up to the gaming floor which is on the first floor is the bank of lifts. We do have stairways, but they are for staff and fire exits. Casino policy stated that anyone being asked to leave had to be escorted in the lifts due to criminal damage and to make sure they actually do leave. The way this worked was pretty straightforward and if it was a weekend and we had enough staff one of us would escort in the lift and we would be met at the bottom by members of our team and we would then walk the person out.

The two guys in question seemed in reasonable spirits and had taken the request to leave with apparent good grace so when they got into the lift with the last of there drinks still in their hand we let them, thinking they could finish them off before we reached the front door. They were amicable and chatty, so I was completely blindsided by what happened, and I learned a very valuable lesson very quickly about trusting punters with drinks. The lift doors closed and immediately the two guys erupted into action. They attacked me trying to hit me with the glasses, both flailing at me as fast as they could. All three of us are over six feet and around the seventeen stone mark, none of us are small. The lifts are maybe five feet by five with a mirror running along the back wall. It was winter, and I had been on the front door until ten minutes ago so luckily for me I was wearing my jacket and a heavy old-fashioned Crombie coat. I threw up my arms tucked my chin into my shoulder and started throwing short rapid punches of my own, keeping my elbows up high and tight I was riding most of the incoming blows while landing a few in the gaps. I managed to latch onto one of them and held his head in a clinch while throwing knees into his ribs. I held my head as tight to his as I could and was pulling him around as a shield, trying to get him between me and his partner. The whole lift ride probably lasted twenty seconds but felt a lot longer as finally the pinging noise sounded, and the doors slid open. The waiting customers quickly jumped back as the three of us bundled out the lift still gripping each other's clothing and throwing short rabbit punches. My colleagues quickly sprung into action and pulled us all apart dragging them to the door. We bundled them out and stood there waiting for the attack which never came. I glared at them as my heart was pounding in my chest, trying to regulate my breathing and regain control after the massive adrenaline dump I had just gone through. Now that they were evenly matched their balls had shrunk and they didn't want to know. I checked myself over and other than skinned knuckles I was unhurt. The lift mirror was cracked, and broken pint glasses littered the floor, but I had somehow escaped with no serious injury again. But I did learn a valuable lesson about trust.

Putting someone to sleep.

I had just punched this guy, and now he was led on the floor unconscious at my feet. He had been threatening and in my face. Posturing up and trying to intimidate me. I had warned him several times to step back, I had tried to make distance and talk him down, but no. He was not going to stop and no amount of trying to appease him was going to work so here we were.

The problem is you can't judge how hard to hit someone. In a situation like this you have to hit them with everything you have, hitting them with only half power will probably just piss them off and get you hurt. And everyone reacts differently. People have different tolerances and pain thresholds, especially if they are chemically enhanced.

We had thrown this guy out for being aggressive. He was giving some lads in the club a hard time and had to go. We had tried to talk to him nicely, but his aggressive nature was not allowing him to see reason, so I had dragged him through the club and out the door away from the other customers. I let him go with a small shove, just enough to get him out of my immediate range. He turned and came straight back at me. He was a big fella, quite muscular with tattooed arms. With my hands up towards his chest to try to manufacture some distance I held him there while he tried to push past. He was showing all the usual signs of a person gearing up for physical, his eyes were staring while he pecked his head forward like a chicken. He kept splaying his arms and pushing his chest towards me. This aggressive posturing was not slowing down and as I tried to reason with him he was not listening. In fact, he was slowly getting worse and his manner became more threatening as he verbalised his intent. All the while he was forcing himself against me, trying to intimidate and crowd me right up until the point I felt that enough was enough.

You need to be very careful judging these moments as hitting anyone carries a risk and even more so for a bouncer as the victim will be the first to run to the old bill because they started it but couldn't finish it. But leaving it to late can get you hurt. I had counted enough justification in my eyes and I was certain he was going to attack me at any moment, so I hit him first.

Bang! From my position with my hands up I threw a short cross punch that I had practised a million times on the heavy bag straight at his jaw. His head snapped back, and he dropped like a stone. My second punch which was already on its way, sailed past where his head used to be. He crumpled onto the floor and lay there unmoving. Shit, I hadn't meant to knock him out and I was surprised such a big guy had fallen so easily. My adrenaline was going mad at this point as I just stood there looking down at my handiwork with my hand throbbing in pain. Maybe ten seconds pass, and the guy lets out a little moan and moves his arm. I let out a long sigh of trapped air, I didn't realise it, but I had been holding my breath the whole time. The guy pushed himself to a seated position and I stupidly asked if he was ok. He pushed himself up to his feet, wobbled a bit and stared at me. I stared back, ready to hit him again if I had to. After glaring at me for a short while he turned without saying a word and walked off into the night.

When nursery rhymes meet violence.

I'm on my door on one of the main streets in Bristol. Park Street is known for it's many bars and clubs and it's also known for violence. Over the years I have worked a number of venues up and down this road and your view of the street will be determined by your venue. Park street is a long straight road that connects Bristol centre via kebab corner to Clifton triangle at the top of the hill. As it climbs up the hill every other building is a club, bar or restaurant and it is just as busy at night as it is in the day. Tonight, I am on my door about a third of the way up the hill. From my vantage point I have a clear view up and down the street. It's quite early and still light and something must be going on as lots of students are out in fancy dress. Being so close to the university meant the clubs would actively target the student population as they were the only ones who could stay out till 4am on a Wednesday and afford it. I'm amusing myself watching the world go by and checking out the different costumes when little Bo Peep walks by. She was wearing one of those ankle-length bell-shaped dresses. The ones with the wire ring support underneath. As it swished from side to side you could just make out little blue bows on the back of her white socks. Her waist was cinched in tight with one of those bodices that laced up the back and a white blouse with puffy shoulders sat underneath it. On her head was a massive bonnet tied to her chin with a ribbon in a large bow. In her hand she carried a shepherd's crook. A crook for those who don't know is a large stick with a hooked end for catching sheep. The nursery rhyme was proving correct as I could not see any sheep nearby. She was with another young girl and they walked past me laughing and chatting as they went.

As they headed down the hill a fast motion caught my eye. A young man of medium build with short dark hair was running downhill, he weaved in and out of the pedestrians before charging across the road straight towards Little Bo Peep. As he came near he raised a fist and threw a running haymaker at the side of her head. The punch connected with a thud as she fell unconscious towards the ground. The running man just kept going and disappeared from view as I jumped from my door and ran towards the girl. I looked down to see her lying in the road, her bonnet was still attached, and a large pool of blood was expanding out from her head. The image of Little Bo Peep lying motionless in her own blood is one that is etched into my brain. Sometimes it would be easier to forget.

8: Fame

I've been on television a few times and once I was even shown on cinema screens up and down the nation. Strange seeing a forty-foot version of yourself, and even stranger getting calls from people all over the place saying they have just seen a giant me while they were tucking into their popcorn. The very first time I was on the tv was in the early 80's. It was a Saturday morning kids programme and they were doing a roadshow with the band Slade playing. For a fleeting glimpse you can see my head and arm in the crowd.

Oddly enough I was asked to appear on a tv show during my first SIA training course to get my certificates. The new badge system had not long come into force and I had been reluctant to do it for personal and family safety issues. My concern was my name. At the time it was emblazoned across the card in big bold letters (it has since been shrunk) and you must wear it in plain sight whenever you are working. The problem I had was that I have an unusual name. In Bristol at the time there were very few listings in the phone book with my name, and only two in the local area therefore making me and my family easy to find if someone decided on some sort of comeback. It made me uncomfortable to think that I could be putting my young son at risk because of my job.

Eventually I had to book a course and get it done so I phoned Bristol college who ran them at the time and booked my place. When I arrived on the first morning to start the course I was met by a camera crew and some female reporter whose name I forget shoving waivers in my face. Apparently, they were there to film a documentary for the BBC based on what it was like to be a female door supervisor. They said they had sought permission from the students prior to the course by mail. Well, no one had contacted me about this and it left me in a bit of an awkward situation as I was already working regularly at that time on some doors and doing some close protection work for people. Not only was I technically breaking the law but what would happen if one of my clients saw me on the show only now receiving my training?

So, I refused. This must have caused them considerable editing issues but hey, that was there problem. The course was run by a short rotund guy whose name I forget. He proudly displayed his shiny badge on a lanyard around his neck for us all to aspire to and told us war stories that I found difficult to believe as his physical presence did not shout tough guy. He also had a strange fascination with fire extinguishers and spoke about them at length with a passion that was evident. As a train spotter gets excited when he sees a new train this guy seemed the same with extinguishers. The course itself passed unremarkably aside from the filming and the only thing of note were some of the fellow students. With me were two young lads who liked to smoke weed in the morning and would arrive with eyes like saucers doing a very credible impersonation of Beavis and Butthead, a guy who rolled up in an Audi convertible with the top down and ridiculously tight designer jeans who loved himself so much I'm sure he went home and licked his own reflection in the mirror. And of course, the ladies who were to be the main feature of the show. Afterwards the presenter was apparently going to shadow a few women working actual shifts to see the job in action. I remember lending her my copy of Geoff Thompson's Watch my back, she never did tell me what she thought of it. The programme was made and shown on the BBC although I have never seen it.

I have also appeared on the show Come dine with me. One of my former students Tony was a contestant and part of his back story showed him getting thrown about by yours truly. Tony is an absolutely lovely guy, but they portrayed him as this smug oily sales type. During the filming it was obvious by the leading questions they were asking him that he would be shown in this manner and when I cautioned him on the fact he wasn't remotely bothered and seemed to be thoroughly enjoying the whole experience.

As you can probably tell by now I am not famous but during my work I have been around many famous people including royalty, actors, comedians, politicians, pop acts and more. It can be one of the great things about this work when you get to meet your heroes, but it can also be a curse when you see behind the façade and realise that they are just people to, and sometimes not nice ones. The magic of film is lost when you have spent fourteen hours a day securing the set and watching the actors between takes sit there in full costume eating a bacon butty. Having worked on several film sets over the years I have seen some very strange sights and asked to look after some even odder things.

While filming for a television series in Bristol we had to secure the set in quite a rough part of town. The series was urban and gritty and the locations were chosen to highlight that. Unfortunately, a percentage of the locals were also urban and gritty and unlike the actors didn't stop with their menacing demeanour when the director shouted cut. We were surrounded by feral kids kitted out in the latest fashions from the sports direct discount rail. These guys were not easily impressed and had many questions they wanted answering and as it was being filmed on their patch felt they could get away with anything. Straight out intimidation and violence would not work as at the first sign of the kids being treated unfairly the entire community would be out in force, so an uneasy truce reigned throughout the filming with us security walking the tightrope, hoping that neither party would say or do something to make the tension erupt. The actors would be delivered to us by shiny white Mercedes where they would go to set and wait their turn. When it arrived, they would step up to the camera and shriek at each other in the style of Eastenders and then vanish again, transported away from the grim reality of where they were, leaving us to sit through the very long hours watching the crew vans and abandoned sets all night.

A little something for the ladies.

There was a time a number of years back when I used to work at the Colston Hall. This is one of Bristol's biggest venues with a long history behind it. A lot of the up and coming acts passed through as did bands slightly past the sell by date. We were not arena tour big as a venue but were lucky sometimes when people would schedule warm up gigs there. I was lucky enough to be on the team when the Stereophonics played a superb set. The money wasn't great, but I got to meet and see loads of bands and it fitted in with my other job. When the shift ended I would race across town to the hotel on the harbourside which would be my home until 6am every weekend. It was here that I learned that pop stars don't always live up to expectation.

It was a typical busy night, the crowds had filtered in and gone to the bar before the show started. This night was an older crowd as the main act was one from the seventies. There star was on the wane, but they could still fill the hall and it was packed out with middle aged couples reliving their youth. As always, an expectant air hung in the room. The support act had warmed them up, those that wanted to had returned to the bar and squeezed one or two more drinks in and now they waited expectantly to be entertained. At the time my position was on the access door to the side of the stage. In it was a round porthole style window in which you could see directly down the corridor to the stage entrance and dressing rooms. But that day I could see something else. There straddling the corridor with one hand pressed against the wall and the other hand shoved down the front of his slightly open tight jeans stood the lead singer. He was having a wank. I couldn't believe what I was seeing and before I could avert my gaze he looked up and made direct eye contact with me. He looked at me for a brief moment, broke out into a big grin and tucked himself in and did his flies up. He then walked up to the door, opened it enough to stick his head through and then spoke to me very casually while still wearing that mischievous grin and said "well, you need to put on a show for the ladies in the front row". It appeared that this was some sort of ritual he did before going on stage. Give yourself a semi to impress the ladies. I have always wondered how many other acts do the same thing. I can't say who it was to avoid any embarrassment, but I have a sneaking suspicion he wouldn't care anyway.

Meet and great.

A singer with one of the most powerful voices is next. He was huge in the eighties with a new romantic band and had gone on to some solo success. I will say right now that the man can sing. If my memory serves me correctly we were doing security for a venue in South Wales which was hosting an early X Factor tour. Chico the goat herder was also on the bill. When Mr Singer turned up I thought he seemed a little drunk, well actually to me he looked pissed. I may be wrong but that is how he seemed. This didn't stop him putting on a hell of a show and at the end I was one of the team tasked to look after him at the backstage door while he signed autographs and had pictures taken. Amongst the group of fifty or so fans all clamouring for his attention one stood out. He was a guy, early thirties who seemed to be a bit out of it. He was pushing into the waiting crowd and repeatedly shouting the singers name. We had repeatedly forced him back and made him move away from the signing area, but he repeatedly tried to push back to the front and was being a complete nuisance. Well this went on for a while and eventually Mr Singer turned to us and told us to let him through. We told him that we thought that was not a good idea, but he said do it. So reluctantly and flanking him very close we allowed this guy near. We would have jumped all over him the minute he showed any aggression. He was still being a dick but our 80's star spoke to him very politely and offered to autograph his jacket. We were thinking wow, he must have the patience of a saint to deal with this sort of thing when he smiled at this idiot and told him to turn around, so he could sign his back. The guy obliged, and he began writing while giving us a big cheesy grin. We didn't understand until the guy straightened up and had the words I am a wanker emblazoned across his jacket. The singer thanked him while patting him on the shoulder and then sent him on his way. I would think he was very annoyed when he finally saw it, but it sure made me and the boys chuckle.

It's my party and I will cry if I want to.

What happens when you get a very famous person fly all the way from his home in LA on his private jet to attend a party all about him and his films and then you have to throw him out?

There's a middle-aged guy stood swaying next to the bar. He is urinating against the panelled wooden front and as it is running down it is pooling around his feet. The other guests have quickly given him space, so he is stood alone in full black tie while around him ladies in cocktail dresses are being ushered away. Normally he would be picked up and carried out the club at this point to be dumped in the street and barred. This situation was a little different as the man in question was a very famous and powerful person. This was his party and he was the reason it was happening. Also, can you imagine the fallout the next morning if we physically throw this guy out dick in hand and the paparazzi get pictures. That would be front page the next day all over the western world. He is an English guy that had found success first here and then across the pond. With his colleagues they had made several very successful films which had led him to the American market. He had now relocated to sunny Los Angeles where he had a sprawling home and a lifestyle that most of us could only wonder at. He had flown back to the UK just for this party, I know this because we had a long chat and he told me. He was due to be in the UK just long enough to attend and then would fly off again.

Maybe it was jetlag, maybe it was all the travel or maybe he was just pissed, I don't know but here we were with this guy with his head down in concentration, blinking and trying to focus in on the pee streaming out of him. We moved forwards and tried to flank him either side without getting in the way of the flow. Taking his arms, we asked him to pull his trousers up and tried to cover him as best we could. We walked him to the back area where I tried to talk to him, given who this guy was diplomacy was required. He wasn't interested in that and this is where I found out all about his travel arrangements and lifestyle. As he told me he kept reminding me that I was just some minimum wage monkey who was never going to achieve anything. He had a plane, he said yet again as he demanded to be allowed back to the main area. The manager had gone to find someone who could deal with this and soon one of the partners arrived. By his reactions I surmised that this sort of thing was not uncommon and within two minutes a driver was summoned, and he was escorted out into the waiting car and away.

He was a fine example of what happens when the only people you have in your circle are yes men. But not all stars are like that.

Meeting God. (the heavy metal version)

Some people I have chosen not to name for fear of embarrassment or even legal repercussions. Some I can name as they turned out to be great people. One of those was the singer Lemmy, from Motorhead. I had actually done concert security for the band a few times but never really met the group, so this was an experience for me as I remember years ago as a kid jumping around and headbanging to Ace of Spades. Like our mate from before Lemmy had also relocated to LA but his travel itinerary was a little different.

This guy walked into the casino alone. It was a quiet night and I was hovering around the lobby. He stood out as he had long hair covered by a cowboy hat, leather trousers and cowboy boots. He came to reception to sign in as all people do and gave his real name, not Lemmy to the lady on the desk. He was rough shaven with a straggly moustache and beard with this huge wart on the side of his face. "You look just like Lemmy" I said to him as he signed it. "I should do" he replied with a grin. Feeling a bit of a dick at this point I wandered back off to circle the lobby some more. Lemmy went off to the gaming floor and sat there quietly playing the fruit machines, occasionally people would go and say hello and he graciously acknowledged each of them. He stayed in the casino for a few hours and then decided to leave. On his way out, he asks if we could get him a taxi. Now the Casino has a deal with a taxi firm that it will only use their taxis and in return get a substantial kickback. As this was the deal we could only use them but sometimes they were less than impressive with their customer service. We sat in the drizzle for twenty minutes talking about stuff, his life and music, the recent tour. I told him about the fact I had done security at some of his gigs and he seemed genuinely interested. After twenty minutes and I have apologised to Lemmy at least ten times for the lack of service I ring the taxi firm back up and hiss at them "we have a fucking genuine legend stood here in the rain. Sort your shit out". I minded more than he did as all he could say was I'm sure it will be here in a minute. Now this is where you see the difference in class between the so-called stars as a week before a ginger haired tv presenter had been in, he had been UK famous for about a year and was demanding we supply him with his own security for his visit. Here we have a 100% rock icon stood in the rain by himself with no entourage happy to chat. When the cab finally arrived he shook my hand, thanked me for passing the time and asked for my name. He then said he would put myself plus one on the VIP guest list for tomorrow night's concert. With that he got in the cab and off they went.

Are Royals famous?

When most people think about bodyguards they usually think of that film with Whitney Houston or the American thrillers where they run alongside the cars. Reality is a little different.

I had received a phone call, members of the Saudi royal family are coming to stay in one of their London residences and would need a team for the duration. It would be a 6- 8 week posting and I was to be paid in crisp £50 notes. That kind of deal is hard to say no to, so myself and two colleagues bundled our limited personal items into the car and we headed off to London. The B&B we were booked into left a lot to be desired and as we were working alternate 12-hour day and night shifts we would share the room and cycle out. It was small and pokey with two single beds that had seen better days, a wardrobe left over from the 70's and above the yellowing washbasin hung a mirror with a large crack running across the bottom half. This was to be our home for the duration and there was nothing glamourous about it. The only positive point is that it was in walking distance of the main house.

The house itself lies in an enclosed area on a private road. Either end of the street is a sentry box and armed Police check-in every vehicle that enters. The grounds back onto one of the British royal family's properties and it was not uncommon to see members of the family being dropped off by helicopter. The entire street housed Diplomats, foreign dignitaries and royalty and I was led to believe that the property and grounds were outside of UK laws.

This was basically a show job, armed police at every corner, members of there own military elite forces accompanied them and some of the worlds most sophisticated security systems were in place. We were there to put on a front and to look good. Truth is I was armed with a dazzling smile and little else, so we were somewhat redundant if anything happened.

I put my suit on, adjusted my tie in the cracked mirror, slid my Crombie coat over my shoulders and took the five-minute walk through the bustling Kensington streets to the staff meeting. I was to run the night shift, we were a team of eight not including their own staff which included SF military, doctors and medical staff, chefs, nanny's, cleaners, and everybody else you can think of including two real life Eunuchs. If you don't know what a Eunuch is it is a man who has had his testicles removed before puberty, so he will never become a man. I believe they used to do this to some opera singers. It is the one and only time I have met men like these and they were the only males allowed onto the female floor of the building.

The family had travelled over in two very large private jets, one for them and one for the staff and supplies. There was also a second house a few doors down which served as the servant's quarters. I had never seen wealth like this before, even the staff's quarters had real gold taps. Everywhere hung fine art and wealth just screamed at you. Think Robbie Williams rich or David Beckham and times it by a thousand. At one point they were bored of the Maybach they were travelling in so dispensed a member of staff to go to there property in Switzerland and bring a different Maybach back with him. One of the princes turned up one day in a high-end supercar with a twist. The car wasn't fast enough or different enough, so he had a plane engine fitted to it. I'm guessing he didn't worry about things like speeding tickets.

Shopping was the favourite pastime and the gates would open as the cavalcade swept past. The OP's (operating procedures) never changed and the radio would crackle into life to start the countdown. All staff were to remain indoors and away from the courtyard as the family would enter and exit. The entry gates would open, and the cars would drive to the front of the house. The driver would walk around the car and open the door as the security team positioned themselves. The family would come out of the main doors walk down the steps and get into the car. Then the second set of gates would be opened, members of the team were placed in the road to stop any oncoming vehicles as the limousine style Maybach's with their blacked-out windows took a wide loop to clear the gates.

All the while the radio would be running through the countdown in my ear. Transport confirmed, 3 vehicles, all recognised. Clear front of house, radio silence for transportation. Gate 1 clear, open gate one. Transport arrived. Close gate 1. Open main doors. Passengers on board. Gate 2 stand by. Gate 2 clear. Open gate 2. Exit clear. Transport away. Close gate 2.

Coming in was the same in reverse and it never deviated. The royal horse guards used to exercise the horses along the road in front and I was always a little concerned that we may try to exit as they were passing. Fortunately, that never happened and things went smoothly.

The night shift was very tedious as most of the family were female they had very strict rules to abide by and had to be in by dark. Occasionally we would be tasked with taking a stroll in the evening sun but most of the time was spent staring at bushes and corridors. We had set positions around the building and house and would rotate every 12 minutes. Round and round we would go for the full twelve hours. Sometimes sleep deprivation would start to kick in and you would feel lightheaded and woozy, I would start to pace furiously at those times, marching backwards and forwards criss-crossing my post and refusing to succumb to the need for sleep.

I learnt a lot in that time about the culture and way of life. Sitting through the night with drivers and cooks and listening to their stories I began to wonder what our real purpose was. All the staff were not from the UK and had their passports withheld from then. The visit here as it turns out is a very hard one for staff management as some of them will try to escape as we in the UK are more tolerant than some other countries. Part of our remit was to keep the staff in and it is quite a scary thought as it almost felt like they were slaves and we were the slave masters tools. I didn't see anyone try to escape although I was informed two did and I wonder if I had seen them would I have stopped them?

9: The fairer sex

It was just another Saturday night. The night was warm and light, and the club was bouncing. It was a lovely summers evening, people were having a good time, and all was well. That was about to change.

I mentioned a young lady earlier in the intro and this is what happened. I was first alerted to her by a scream. The entrance to the club led right onto one of the busiest streets in Bristol. Along the length are bars and clubs and lots of people were milling along the pavements. The customers from our club came in and out and joined the steady flow. We were busy, so we had a constant stream of people entering and leaving. We heard the scream just away from our door. I looked up from the queue to see a young man with blood gushing from the side of his face. He had his hand held to the side of his head and the blood pumped through his fingers and blossomed across one side of his crisp white shirt. A young lady nearby was shrieking continuously, and onlookers gathered, looking at the spectacle in a mixture of horror, confusion and fascination. Among them was a young women. She appeared to be about 20. She was very pretty with a petite slim figure and mid length blonde hair. She was stood completely rigid. She remained still and just stared at the guy, never taking her eyes off him. In her hand was a broken beer bottle which had little droplets of blood that dripped from the jagged edges and made a small puddle on to the pavement. We quickly went to intervene, so I took the lad and guided him towards the club entrance where we went inside and sat him down on a side bench to assess the damage. His face was ashen, and he seemed confused. Gently I encouraged him to slowly move his hand, as he did so a great flap of skin from forehead to jaw slowly peeled away from his face. The skin now sticky with blood flapped loose and another surge of fresh blood started to run off his chin. One of the staff handed me a wad of paper towels so we got him to hold them against his face to try and stem the flow. He was obviously in shock and his brain was having serious issues with trying to catch up with the events of the last few minutes. Repeatedly I had to tell him to keep still as he kept trying to take his hand away. Every time he did his own face would flap down into his line of vision and he kept trying to look at it to process in his mind what he was seeing. The paper towels quickly became soaked and had to be replaced and although the paramedics were on the way time distortion kicked in and minutes felt like hours.

The young lady that had bottled him. She was his ex-girlfriend. They had been in a relationship and for reasons unknown had split up recently. Independently and by chance they had both decided to enjoy the night in my club. I don't know at which point the ex became aware of the new couple and how long she sat there. He had met a girl and they were out on a date, as far as he was concerned his ex was old news and he was moving on. As the young couple flirted, giggled, and kissed the ex watched from a distance. Resentment grew, how dare he be here with someone new. Why should he be happy and why should that bitch be allowed to touch her man. She sat and brooded, all thoughts of enjoying her night gone. At some point their eyes met and when he realised that his ex was here the young man whispered to his date that they should leave. He did not want a scene and as the night was still young they could go to another venue and enjoy the rest of the evening.

She saw them start to make their way out and got up to follow, on the way she picked up an empty beer bottle that the busy bar staff had yet to collect. She held it against her body and hid it with her arm. The club policy was that no drinks were allowed outside the venue. The ex knew this so concealed it as she followed the couple through the bar and out of the entrance. As they got to the street she moved closer and then shouted his name. As he turned towards her she swung the bottle towards his face. Blindsided he didn't even attempt to block it and the glass connected with the side of his head partially breaking and slicing downwards from his temple. Did she intend to do the damage she caused? I couldn't say, but it was one of the nastiest injuries I have seen, and it was done by a petite young woman that looked like the proverbial girl next door.

Expert in a week.

The club was banging, the music pumped out and the party crowd were in full swing. It was around midnight and the busiest time at this venue. We were open into the small hours and this was the time a lot of clubbers would turn up. To the left of the double doors we had a long line of punters snaking down the side of the building waiting to get in, all chattering and excited. To the right a semi-enclosed smoking area that was entered via a separate door by our customers that were already in the venue. That night we only had three doorstaff on and were caught a little off guard as to how popular tonight's promotion was going to be. We were virtually at compacity with a line of people eager to get through the door. Working that night was myself, Sharon, and Ed. I was the head door and it was my club. I was the regular face and the punters knew me. Ed had worked here a few times. He was a student type but with a big build. He stood maybe 6,3" but was not a fighter. Sharon was a tall, over skinny lesbian in her mid-thirties. I'm not sure, but I think she lived in a van. She had that pinched look as if she was scowling at everything. She didn't seem to like men very much. I don't mean in a sexual way, I mean in general.

She had also recently completed the training needed to teach the door supervisors course. After a week of very basic physical intervention training she had become an extremely annoying know it all and so-called expert on all things violent. She never managed to get a job teaching those skills though as no-one took her new-found expertise seriously. We had asked for more staff and were hoping we could pull someone from another venue soon. A young black guy stepped to the front of the queue, he wore a vest and joggers, on his head was one of those NY caps and he sported a thick gold chain around his neck and another around his wrist. He had no ID so the guys went into the usual spiel. No ID, no entry. If you looked under 25, proof of age was necessary at this club. But if you go and get some we can let you in. Matey boy was not happy with this and tried to plead his case. This was going on for quite a few minutes. Meanwhile the queue had slowed to a snail's pace as my colleagues tried to deal with him, no-one was monitoring the interior and the music continued to thump as the mc spat. He realised this was getting him nowhere so changed tack. He became abusive. Ed and Sharon tried to use their conflict management skills, but matey boy wasn't having it. Spurred on by the onlookers he decided to become threatening. Meanwhile the queue is blocked, and we are short staffed. As head doorman I was monitoring the whole picture so had stayed back as the situation was being dealt with. That was until it outgrew them. This guy pushed Sharon and hurled abuse. I rushed forward. Sharon staggered back, Ed just looked confused. I shot forward grabbed matey boy by his arm and gold chain and executed a scruffy hip toss. His legs went from under him and as he span in mid-air he grabbed out in a reflexive action and grabbed onto my jacket. The grab reflex is a subconscious response we all have when we lose our balance. Its why if you watch a judo match there are very few clean throws, more often it will end in a pile of bodies as it did with us. I had flipped matey boy onto his back, but he had pulled me down with him. I pushed off him and came to a knee, he grabbed out with the other hand and was trying to drag me to the floor. The smokers were watching now with interest. Fearing a grappling match on the floor amongst the smashed glass and fag butts I hooked my thumb under his jawbone where it reaches the corner to move up towards the ear. Digging my thumb in and twisting as hard as I could. I was also at this point kneeling on his belly, pushing my bodyweight into his ribs. I was trying to force him to let go by creating pain as I knew the point where I was jamming my thumb is very sensitive. Sharon meanwhile had obviously recovered from her push and instantly forgotten it as she decides to start yelling in a high pitched excited squeal "you can't choke him, that's not allowed. Take your hands off his throat". She is shouting this in front of our customers while neither Sharon nor Ed move. I explained in hissed tones that she was not helping and to shut the fuck up. Matey boy meanwhile was squirming underneath me on the hard pavement. With a final twist I managed to force his head back, so he lost his grip on my clothes. I rolled him face down and pinned him, explaining loudly that I didn't want to hurt him and that he needs to calm down. Unusually in these situations two police officers just happened to come around the corner. They looked at the situation and arrested matey boy. After a quick scan of the cameras they were happy that I had acted within the law and that was that, just another day at the office. But it wasn't for Sharon. After her little outburst I sacked her from the venue and refused to ever work with her again. She was and probably still is a fucking liability.

Stilettos

I learnt very early on to be wary of the fairer sex. The poem may say sugar and spice but when you add alcohol and drugs into the mix that doesn't end in all things nice. This was a very steep learning curve I was on. This was one of my first shifts, I had not been working very long and was still very unsure of how to deal with things. I was greener than grass and more innocent than a good catholic girl.

This evenings shift was at a working man's venue in a working man's part of town. As a newbie I had been told to stand there and monitor the interior while the guys ran the front. The bar was long, in an L shape, against the wall running alongside the bar were grubby bench seats and at the end a bank of fruit machines which intermittently would flash and light up to tempt in the bored and the gamblers. Around the corner was a back room that housed a pool table. This is where a lot of the local dealing was done. This was the locals equivalent of an office and stolen goods were offered and drugs and cash went back and forth in a separate economy that only the working class really know about. I was watching all of this going on with a kind of detached boredom. You as a reader may at this point think why wasn't I stopping any of this? My answer is simple. It goes on in pubs up and down the length of the country, always has and always will. In that kind of place, you mostly turn a blind eye as you can't stop it and truth is the landlord and locals don't want you to.

So, I find myself witnessing the scene that unfolded in front of me. Two of the locals, a couple. Think Jeremy Kyle audience and you are not far wrong. Skinny, ashen faced and tattooed. They both looked in need of a good sleep and a good meal. He was sporting the latest line of fake named brands, she was wearing a dress where her bony hips protruded out and showed the faded tattoo of a dolphin on the top of her breast. Words were spoken between the two, it became animated and then quickly erupted. He grabbed her by her shoulder length hair and head butted her straight into her nose. Her nose exploded as it flattened across her face, blood spattered through the air as she was knocked back. She staggered hit the pool table and hunched herself down holding her face with her knees tucked up tight in a seated foetal position, cowering from his wrath. My guess is this is not the first time she has been a victim. I ran forward grabbed him by the shirt front with both hands and ran him backwards into the wall. His head ricocheted off the nicotine stained wallpaper to be met by my forearm. I jammed my arm under his chin and forced his head back, pinning him. I could hear the barmaid yelling for my colleagues who were on the front door. My back was turned away from the girl during this time, so It came as quite a shock to suddenly feel a searing pain in my head. She had seen me grab the guy and slam him into the wall and for whatever reason had decided to defend him. She got up from the floor, using the pool table to help her rise. Then she removed one of her stiletto shoes, held it like a club. Rushing to his aid she ran towards me bringing it down onto the top of my head where the heel imbedded itself into my flesh. She was yelling "get off him. You're hurting him, he aint done nuffink" as she flailed away at me with her shoe. I swung round and pushed her. Sending her careening back to her position on the floor by the pool table. My colleagues arrived, and we dealt with the situation, but the moral of the story is, never turn your back on a woman.

The chicken and the feet.

I was asked one day to cover a shift. It was a venue I didn't know but had heard about. It came with a reputation and its own health warning. It was one of those places surrounded by high rise flats that loomed upwards into the sky. Satellite dishes protruded from them at weird angles like the building had caught a disease. Barbed wire surrounded the rooftops of the shops and the corrugated pull-down shutters were decorated with graffiti and gang tags. The venue was known as a hotbed of theft and drugs. You could go in and speak to a scaghead and they would go and steal it for you to order, and you would pay half price. There's a tale of one of our guys who was sitting on the loo minding his own business when all of a sudden, a head appeared over the top of the cubicle. The mouth split into a smile showing the gaps where teeth used to be. A frozen chicken was being waved back and forth by one of the locals and the question was asked" do you want to buy a chicken for a quid?"

There's a group of people sat in the bar around a table. One of the group is a woman in her 50's. Maybe she's younger but life has kicked her in the arse so much its added years to her. She is squeezed into a pair of black leggings. You know the ones, pulled tight across an acre of ass, becoming almost see through under the pressure of all that bulk. The gusset was starting to fray, and holes were appearing at the seams. To my absolute horror she is sat in the chair barefoot. One of those feet is in her hand and in between swigs of lager, loud guffaws, and stories of her down the road, you know the one. She is bringing her foot to her mouth and hunching forward, then ripping off pieces of toenail with her teeth. She is then looking over her shoulder and spitting the piece of toenail out where it sails across the room to land indiscriminately among the tables. Not all ladies are ladies I have found.

Would you do that sober?

It's Saturday night again, the weeks roll past in a blur and we are once again in the hot sticky summer evenings. Tonight, has been a busy one on the door, the club we are on is low ceilinged with little ventilation and no windows. The punters were crammed in and sweated, drank, sniffed, and swallowed everything they could lay their hands on. The smoking area was through the front door and as it was so hot even the non-smokers were coming out repeatedly just to cool off. We were probably just as busy outside as we were inside the club with a pretty even distribution of customers.

One young lady had been in and out all night. A young pretty blonde, with tanned legs high heels and a tiny dress that just about covered her arse cheeks. She was in the party spirit and every time she reappeared at the door she was a little worse than the time before. As she was getting more inebriated and less in control we were keeping an eye on her and had already spoken a few times. She, like a lot of women didn't want to wear the shoes she had chosen to bring out. Apparently, they looked great with that dress but were a bitch to walk in. Her words. We had a policy in the club that footwear must be worn at all times, and as she approached to come back in once again her heels were in her hand. She slurred and rocked as she tried to comprehend that she needed to put her shoes back on. At this point we were aware she was getting to the point of being too drunk but as it was us that had sold her the alcohol to get that way and she had friends in the venue we were reluctant to throw her out in the street on her own and vulnerable.

I repeated the words "you need to put your shoes on to come back in". The lightbulb went off and the message had sunk in. "OK" she said and tried to lift her leg up. That wasn't happening and as she wobbled and hopped trying to hook a foot with her shoe she overbalanced and crumpled downwards into an untidy sitting position on the curb side. Not to be defeated she rocked forward and grabbed her leg at the ankle, with her other hand brandishing the shoe she attempted to bring them together. The effort was working as she hooked her shoe over her toes, as she tried to pull it over her foot she overbalanced and rocked backwards still holding her leg.

An interested murmur came from the packed smoking area as the young lady was not wearing underwear and as she rocked back she exposed herself to everyone watching. She rocked back and forward fighting with her shoe flashing herself every time she rocked back. The smokers started to cheer her and then boo us as we tried to sit her up. She was angrily batting our hands away as we tried to protect her modesty. Trying to hold her while her legs are in the air with everything hanging out was no easy task as she was like an irate upturned turtle. We managed to right her to a sitting position and helped her to put her shoes on. As we did so we explained that she was giving the guys a free show and with no shame or embarrassment she said, "so what?"

10: Sex and come-on's

If you let me in I will give you a blow job. Give me the blow job and if it's any good I might.

It's amazing what a difference three feet can make to a woman's attitude towards you. As the gatekeepers to the clubs and bars we are often given a lot of female attention. Mostly its just because they want to get in. They will flirt outrageously, batting their eyelashes and stroking your arm, accidently on purpose brushing their tits against you. They will giggle and laugh and tell you you have a nice smile or big muscles while they give you their undivided attention. For that moment you appear to be her best friend and who knows what else in the future. You let them in the door and they have no need for you anymore. Now you are dead to them, try talking to them inside and you will be blanked and greeted with the gesture for talk to the hand.

Then there are the doorman fanciers, if you think about it we tick a lot of boxes, we are dressed smartly in a type of uniform, we have a perception of power and a lot of ladies like to feel protected. Which means quite often you would get attention from the ladies. When I was younger I made full use of this fact, but the truth is its not you they are interested in, it's the persona. It's the picture of the bouncer that they have drawn in their mind. And then to make it worse if you do start dating its not long before they are nagging you to pack the doors in and get a real job. Very few women are able or willing to cope with a new relationship where you are working every weekend and surrounded by just the sort of women that she was a few shorts weeks ago. They have a really tough time coping with that one.

Sex sells, from the girls thrusting there tits forward to get served at the bar quicker to the lap dancing clubs where lonely businessmen and stag parties pay to get a hard-on. Women are aware of the power they hold, and men are perpetually stupid when it comes to them.

Movie stars.

There was a barmaid once called Anna who worked in a pub that is situated in the middle of a large edge of town council estate. The area is run down, forgotten by local government, and rotted from years of under investment. The pub was mostly full of locals and you could buy pretty much anything you wanted out of the boot of a car in the car-park. The black market was the economy here, and the shoplifters went out to order, local dealers sat round the pool tables constantly texting and sending the kids to meet the cars that would pull up at the front of the pub. Everyone had a scam; disability fraud was rife and working cash in hand was the order of the day. Anna also had her ways of making a little extra money.

Anna would meet unsuspecting guys, she was no spring chicken and her best years were behind her, but she still carried the remnants of a figure and when it was all squeezed into that little black dress it mostly stayed in the right places. The unsuspecting guy would think Christmas had come early when she would sidle up and whisper that their luck was in and tonight they were going to be going home with her. She would uphold her end of the bargain, back they would go to her council flat and perform all kinds of tricks. Her enthusiasm knew no bounds and there was no act or position that those lucky guys could dream up that she wouldn't oblige them with. The thing is unknown to them nestled amongst the teddy bears and cushions was a video camera and Anna made films. They unwittingly became porn stars in her home-made movies which she would then sell to anyone that wanted a copy. The locals knew this and generally stayed clear but there was always somebody that didn't and the first they knew of it was when they saw themselves or were told by someone they know that they were a star. I'm sure there are many guys out there who have been in these home-made films that still don't know. They probably sit in their local pub somewhere around the country bragging to their mates out of earshot of the wife how they shagged this bird when they were working away in Bristol. Little do they realise that somewhere out there, people are watching them.

The boyfriend conveyer belt.

I am working in the hotel tonight. This one looks over Millennium square with the big silver sphere in front. It's a one-man door and I am here till six am. This particular hotel chain has two properties in the city and this one is where they send the party goers and the stag dos. The other one is where the businessmen and families go. They have a nice quiet relaxed atmosphere away from the alcohol fuelled madness, while I am surrounded by naked men letting off fire extinguishers, large groups fighting, sex in the public areas and many other crazy things. It really is a modern-day Sodom and Gomorrah on a Saturday night and it is only made worse by the website offering a twenty-four-hour bar. You only book into a hotel with a twenty-four-hour bar for certain reasons. A large bulk of bookings are on the night and people will regularly come in having recently pulled wanting a room for nothing more than to go and have sex. The hotel is fully aware of this and at our partner hotel you cannot walk in and book on the night. Here however you can and as we were a two-minute walk from one of the biggest nightclubs in Bristol we were never short of people showing up on a promise.

It was probably around midnight and the double glass doors swished open as a young couple walked in. They were arm in arm and very tactile. In between long sloppy kisses where I'm sure they were sucking the fillings out of each other's teeth they were trying to book a room. The cheapest on offer if I remember rightly was about £40 which they had to pay for right then. It turns out that they had a slight problem as a card was also needed and as they finally stopped kissing to figure it out the two lovebirds formed a plan. She had a card but no money on it, in fact she had spent all her money getting to this stage. He had money but no card as he apparently didn't believe in credit cards. That's what he told her as she handed her card over for the receptionist to scan. She then took the money and handed them a card key. With that the snogging recommenced and they staggered off to the lifts.

Less than half an hour later the couple are back. They get out of the lift and this time the atmosphere between them is quite different. They are hurling abuse at one another, according to her he's a dim-witted bell end who needs to go back to his mother, he retorts back with "Fuck off bitch". They continue to have a blazing row in the lobby and swear words are being dropped like bombs for all our other guests to hear. I intervene and ask them to calm down and take it elsewhere as its bothering the other guests. The pair then go out of the front doors and just around the corner continue the argument in full swing. Everyone in the bar can see them through the large panelled windows that run the full length of the wall as they gesticulate, point and stamp their feet. After about five minutes of this the male storms off across the square as she throws her cigarette butt to the floor, stamps on it then makes her way back to the lift.

Fifteen minutes go by and the lady is back. The lift doors open and out she walks. She too then disappears across the square. Good, I thought to myself they were a pain the arse. About an hour has gone by and as I am gazing out from the lobby who should be back? It's the girl from earlier but this time she has another guy with her. Although it's not the same guy they are doing the same things as they disappear into the lift snogging and groping each other's arses. I shake my head and carry on with doing nothing as it's a slow night.

Another hour or two goes by and the first guy rocks back up. I wake up a little at this as it may get interesting. He walks through our glass doors as they automatically part on his arrival and makes his way to reception. He asks the receptionist for a key to his room. Now there are two main problems with this, one is the girl who he got the room with originally is now occupying it with another guy. The second is that as it was her card it is registered too technically it is not his room even though he paid for it. The receptionist very politely tried to explain to the gentleman that he could not have a key as it was not his room, which was starting to piss him off as he couldn't understand the concept of this. It was his money he argued. He then said he would just go up to the room. Obviously, that was not going to end well so I had to intervene at this point and try to clarify the situation. I figured it would be unwise to mention the other guy, but I still enflamed his anger when I tried to explain that only registered guests were allowed on the floors. He was getting increasingly frustrated by the minute and with it his anger was rising. I could totally understand his frustration and genuinely felt sorry for the guy but there was nothing we could do so when I had to physically coax him towards the doors it was done with little conviction. He stood and argued his point for well over an hour. I actually felt sorry for him and could see his point of view perfectly. He had paid for the room but yet couldn't stay in it and as he kept pointing out he had no money for another.

The sun had started to come up. The loud squawking of the seagulls filled the air as they worried the kebab wrappers that overflowed from the bins. Here and there dishevelled party goers were mooching along home while others just sat in doorways, completely underdressed for the crisp air that came with the dawn. The guy who couldn't get into his room had found a place to sit opposite the hotel and was sat on his jacket chain-smoking and watching the doors. All was normal until the girl reappeared out of the lifts holding hands with boyfriend number 2. As the lobby was wide open and windows ran along the walls he could see them from his vantage point as they appeared from the lift. Grabbing his jacket, he ran across the street and as the couple stepped out into the morning air he hit boyfriend 2 with a haymaker of a right hand knocking him to the ground. He then sat over him and started throwing punches. My shift had just ended when this happened, and I had just finished signing out in the back office. I walked round reception to see this guy sat astride the other guy. Reception were already calling the police, so I ran over and separated them. The girl seemed to think it was funny and was goading them both, so I told her to shut the fuck up. Boyfriend 1 was angry and wanted to paste this guy. Boyfriend 2 was confused. He knew nothing about number 1. He had just been out having a good time, met this girl who appeared very keen. Then she proved it by taking him to the hotel room. And now he was going to just do the walk of shame like so many others. He had no idea boyfriend number 1 existed and was not anticipating being attacked on leaving. Unfortunately for boyfriend number 1 the police turned up, and he was carted off. What a shit night he had. His missus nearly shags him, he then can't get into the room he paid for and can't afford another, his missus is using that room to shag someone else, and then he gets nicked.

The perv with the matching face.

The lad was rudely pushed to the ground, He had been dumped there by the guys. The head doorman pointed down at him and told him "you better fuck off before you really get battered". With that the lad got up and ran off into the crowds of the busy city centre.

This is another bar that in its day was very popular with the clubbers, it would be full to bursting every weekend and could get a bit punchy. It was a popular chain bar situated smack bang in the city centre. Right outside were rows of bus stops that would ferry the drinkers to the centre from the local estates all around the city. As such it was a popular meeting point but would also get some friction due to the groups of lads from different areas all coming together.

A week had gone by since this lad had been thrown out and it was another busy Saturday evening. A taxi pulled up and four heavyset builder types got out. They walked towards the door not smiling but maintaining eye contact. This didn't feel like they were coming for a night out. As they reached the door we stepped together to form a barrier across the door blocking entrance. The leader snapped at the HD "which one of you fuckers smacked up my boy last week? Tell me which one of you so-called hard men done it and we will have a go. I'll fucking do you". The group were all crowding in, menacing and threatening and it looked like a war was about to erupt. I had lined up my guy and was going to hit him as hard as I could the moment it went live, but the HD said quite calmly "Do you mean the dark-haired lad in the white shirt from last week?" "Yes" said Dad starting to square up. "Come with me" replied the head doorman "if you still want to fight at the end I will fight you, but let me show you something first". He took the guy inside while we maintained an uneasy truce with the remainder of the group, steered him through to the back and replayed the footage from last week. Dad made his way back through the club and out through the doors, without stopping he just kept walking. His group were left with no choice but to hurry after him as he marched off.

Another week had gone by and another Saturday night was upon us when who should be heading towards us but the lad from two weeks ago. His face was a riot of colour, down one side was the deep purples and browns of older bruises sustained when he tried to fight the HD when he was thrown out. The other side of his face was also bruised. But these were fresher, and his cheek and eye were still puffy and swollen. We were unsure what to expect so our greeting was guarded. He explained that he was here to apologise to us. His father on seeing the footage had gone back home and with the uncles they had given this lad another pasting. That explained the bruises. They then insisted he personally come to the door and apologise to the team and assure them he would never come to that bar again.

When dad was shown the footage, he looked down at the black and white version of his son and slowly the realisation of what he was seeing sunk in. His son had undone his flies and pulled his dick out. In a very crowded bar where people were pushed up against each other and had to squeeze through the crowds he was moving through rubbing his cock on the unsuspecting women as he went. He had been caught red-handed in the act and as he was being taken out had tried to punch our HD who at the time was a family man in his 40's and had daughters, so you can imagine the willpower it took not to really batter this kid. Instead he gave him one short straight to the side of the head and then threw him in the street. Dad on the other hand was not so controlled and gave the lad a right kicking.

How rough is too rough?

It's a normal night on the square, the madness of the clubs closing has started to die down and the foot traffic has become less and less. This is quite often a good time. A time to reflect, daydream and stare at the large shiny sphere in the corner of the square. I have still never been inside it, so I must add that to my bucket list after staring at it for so many years. I have a few hours to kill to the end of my shift at six. As a way to stay awake I go and do a lap of the building, anything to stop my eyelids from starting to droop. Sometimes you would prefer something to happen just to wake you up and get you through the night.

Well something did happen. I had done my walk round and stepped out into the pre-dawn night as the automatic doors slid open in front of me. I had a cigarette in my mouth (back when I used to smoke) and as I reached up with my lighter my eyes were drawn to a scene on the other side of the road. Pushed down over one of those grit boxes you see that are normally yellow was a slightly overweight women. Her chubby white thighs were being held up by a guy. He had pushed her panties to one side and was smacking her round the head with his free hand while he thrust away making her butt jiggle. He was calling her a dirty slut and fucking bitch and as I ran towards them I could hear her mumbling. A colleague from a neighbouring venue had also run to join me as we confronted the pair. My first thought was that he was raping her as that is exactly what it looked like. I grabbed him and pulled him away while the women pulled her skirt down and tried to cover up. I admit to being a little rough as I was thinking the worst. I put my face up close to his while holding him by the throat and demanded he tell me what the fuck was going on.

He tried to draw breath and clawed at my hands as he blurted out its not what you think. I eased my grip a little, still suspicious and resisting the urge to choke him some more. He told me they were role-playing and that's how they got their jollies. She liked it rough and was a willing participant in this. I asked my colleague to take him to one side while I repeatedly asked the girl if this was true. My fear was that she wasn't telling the truth for whatever reason, but she insisted that it was consensual.

Turns out for these guys at least, play acting being raped was sexy!

Famous fanny.

Tonight, I find myself front of stage. Grace Jones has just hula-hooped her way through an entire song. My job for tonight was to work the pit and the front of stage for the legendary singer, actress and man-eater that is Grace Jones. I first remember seeing her in a Bond movie and one of the Conan films. Her persona of a very abrupt, physical person is not fake. That is exactly how she is, and the years had not softened the edges. I must admit she makes me nervous. But on with the show. We are in the pit area looking out at the audience that are enthusiastically singing along and having a great time. I really only know one maybe two of Miss Jone's songs but even in her 60's she is putting on a show. The stage behind me is raised to just past my waist height and the speakers are spread intermittently along the front directly in line with my head so I am getting a very loud distorted version of her greatest hits. She is very active and as usual not wearing a lot, prowling around the stage like a caged beast and letting out guttural noises in between song lyrics. At times her voice goes very deep and almost masculine. One of the things she is known for in her shows has just happened and for the entirety of the song she rotated a hula hoop around her midriff.

I am stood with my back to the stage, hands clasped in front of me as I look out over the audience when I feel a hand touch the top of my head. Grace Jones is stood behind me trying to dry hump the back of my head. The realisation hits hard, I am now part of the show as Grace growls and grinds behind me, her hand trying to pull me into her thrusting crotch. I quickly pull away and step a few paces down the stage. Miss Jones stands up puts her hand between her legs, looks me full in the face and announces into the mike "you don't know what you are missing".

She then went back to her set and finished the show. The next day the Evening post reported on the concert and mentioned the exchange although they misrepresented what happened as I assume the reporter misheard exactly what was said.

Very few people scare me the way Grace Jones did.

A round of applause please.

Today I am at a disused private airfield. The land has been hired for a corporate event. Amongst the attendees will be work colleagues from the company and students from the local university. The event has had a lot of money put into it and the entertainment includes fairground rides and a live music stage. Obviously, there is a bar and lots of other stalls to help the party along. It was a good day and lots of people arrived by cars while more came via coaches. As this was on an abandoned airfield it was too far to walk. The day moved on without incident and everyone seemed to be having a good time. We mingled with the customers and chatted to the stall holders. Ever the fair rides were pretty well behaved which is unusual as these can quite often get a bit rowdy as the alcohol flows.

The day went well, and it was time for everyone to leave and close-up the site. This time of day is always tough as we have been on our feet for hours and now want it to be over, the punters however are enjoying themselves and want to eek out every extra second they can. The coaches are lined up waiting to collect the passengers and the stallholders are packing away stock as we sweep the site to clear everyone. The site is in the middle of a large open space and as I walk the perimeter I hear noises coming from the darkness. I shine my torch in the direction and there in the darkness are two young students making the most of the moment. It is obvious they are having sex, so I shine the light away and loudly announce the coaches are leaving in two minutes. I hoped this would hurry them up as I continued my round of the site. When I got to the coaches I was told one of them could not leave as it was missing two passengers. The other coaches pulled away as the bus load of party goers stared out into the darkness impatiently waiting for the two lovers. I walked back to where they were last seen, and they were still there locked together. We shouted out again that it was time to wrap it up and shone torches in the general direction. Still no response besides the grunts of passion. Word had reached the coach as to where the missing people where and some of the passengers got off and started heading to the scene. Again, we tried to ask the guys to get dressed and come back. As some of the students started arriving on the field more and more torches and phone lights were pointed at the couple on the ground. They had moved position now and he was kneeling on the floor thrusting forward in the vinegar strokes, face contorted with the effort. She was on her back in front of him, legs straight up tight to his chest with her ankles either side of his head writing on the floor. In the light of a dozen or so spectators they reached the finale of the little show. He stood and put his trousers on while she readjusted her short dress and pushed her tits back into her bra. Both then calmly walked towards the coach. When they got to there they climbed the steps onto the bus to be met with a cheering standing ovation.

11: Martial arts

I am lucky in that I found martial arts. They have allowed me to meet some fantastic people, see the world, achieve goals, and become a better person. When I was younger I never liked team sports and never understood the urge to all jump in a bath together naked at the end. What I understood less was the fact you could train as hard as you could, do everything right and still lose because of someone else's efforts or lack of. Paradoxically, people can claim a glory that isn't there's. Shout of someone else's achievement as if it was their own. Martial arts and the fighting disciplines are not like that, you win or lose on your own actions. The only one who can take the credit is the one who deserves it. You stand there alone, and you face an opponent of relative size and ability and on the day, you were better than that person. It is as honest and raw as it gets.

The fact that in martial arts you really can get to meet and become friends with your heroes is still a sense of wonder to me and to have the ability to drink a cup of tea and chat with or call up people I used to admire on film and in magazines is something that I treasure for the gift that it is. Let me put this in perspective. If you are a football fan and your heroes are Ronaldo or Rooney, what are the chances of you getting to have a kick about with them? Or maybe a quick call to ask about a way of tackling that turns into an hour-long conversation? I would say you had more chance of waking up next to Cameron Diaz and Kylie Minogue, both naked and holding tubs of whipped cream telling you that Angelina Jolie will be back in a minute. But in the martial arts you can.

I encourage everyone to try some form of training as it can bring so many benefits in all areas of life but for anyone looking into getting into security I would say you need to. With fightclubs and gyms popping up on every street and blackbelts on every corner you need to keep up. One of the downsides to the modern world is in the old days it took years of dedicated training before you were taught the good stuff. Now people with nothing more that a surface knowledge of what they are doing are getting a full sleeve, wearing a man bun, and applying rear naked chokes to each other the length and breadth of the country. A kid can walk into a gym nowadays and be on the mats practising murdering each other within the hour. You need to stay ahead of the knowledge curve.

I have practised and studied many arts over a long period of time and I have seen the fads as the latest devastating martial art becomes fashionable and then fades as something else explodes in popularity and all the fanboys claim it to be the only martial art that really works. My version is this. I think that every single art has value and every single person that trains will have individual reasons for doing so and as long as the two are in synch then that is great. What boils my piss and makes me incandescent with rage is certain groups claiming the synchronised dance they perform will save somebody in a real encounter. We in this industry are horribly under-regulated and any idiot can claim almost anything, and in the main get away with it. Consumer rights don't count in the same way as in the real world. Imagine if you went to the supermarket and asked for a yogurt and they said, we don't have one of those but here's a pork pie it's the same thing. That supermarket would be breaking the law. But in the world of martial arts many people are peddling there wares as real or street lethal and some even believe their own nonsense, some it seems have turned into cults. All arts to me have good and bad points and its identifying those that is the key. As a bouncer that needs skills that are really going to be usable I must ask some honest questions. What would help in this environment? And what would get me hurt? I have seen a guy throw on a full rear naked from his back on a punter, both hooks in, right in the middle of the dancefloor.

Technically it was awesome until the guys mate kicked him in the head like he was taking a penalty and knocked him out cold. Or the guy that went in for a double-leg on a hard-concrete pavement. As his knee connected with the tarmac and the guys weight fell on top of him he screamed in agony as his Kneecap shattered. Or the boxer whose sitting in jail for excessive use of force because punching people was all he knew, and the punter ended up with his jaw broken in three places.

The truth is most arts get a bad name because of the idiots that go around picking fights in bars claiming to be an expert in this or that and are normally full of shit. I have seen it myself, more than once. The genuinely scary ones with the real knowledge are almost without exception the nicest people you could wish to meet.

Being a blackbelt means I'm hard, right?

Many times, over the years I have worked with martial artists and the truth is, if you have a blackbelt in an art you are more likely to be given a chance on the doors. There is a perceived level of competence that comes with the rank that is sometimes horribly misplaced.

We will call him Darren for the sake of the story. Darren did martial arts and made sure everyone knew about it. At every opportunity he would barge his training into the conversation and loudly proclaim that while everyone else was still in bed he was up doing 100 knuckle press-ups. He was new to doorwork and had been given the start as he held a third-degree black belt in a quasi-traditional sporting system and had won a few medals. So, we had to listen to him regal us with stories of his many and varied street fights where he was so deadly every (imaginary) encounter ended in him knocking his adversary's unconscious.

For those who don't do martial arts or maybe follow a different way let me draw you a picture of how his medals were won. First, he joined a club. At that club he was made to wear certain clothes, a uniform used especially for this style of fighting, and a lot of the movement required the person to wear one for it to work. Next, he would have to bow on entering the sacred village/school/sports hall and then bow again to his seniors. His seniors would be given honorific titles and wear symbols of their expertise. These people were given total respect. Next, he would need to use a foreign language. His local club is 3 miles from his house, but he must learn and use the correct terminology. Finally, he would be taught how to fight. This was done in a number of ways, first he and his fellow students would line up in rows and punch and kick into the unresisting air. Emitting a loud shout on the exhale as they twisted the wrist at the exact moment for the correct knuckle alignment. Then they would learn a series of moves. They would memorise them and perform them alone in a kind of moving meditation. This is designed to help the student to learn the fighting art of the system. Finally, they would fight. Now when I say fight I mean spar, and in a very specific way. All martial art styles that do competition have to apply rules for everyone's safety. What those rules are differ from style to style. First there is a ref and a time limit, the opponents meet on a well lit matted floor. Both are wearing headguards, gumshields, chest protectors, forearm guards, gloves, groin guards, shin pads and feet protectors. Both are told they can only perform allowed techniques, about 10% of what was in the choreographed sequence of moves they learned, and both are told that they cannot strike full power and can only hit scoring areas. With this the ref makes them bow to him and then to each other, they then face each other at the prescribed distance. Finally, after all that the ref will shout go in the language of choice and the two combatants will move into the range of whatever style they are competing in and try to score a point.

Now the guy at the front door wasn't interested in belts or medals, in fact was interested in nothing but beating Darren a new head. This guy was 6'2 and thick set, hands calloused from a lifetime of manual work. His shoulders and upper back pushed his t-shirt tight and the many tattoos on his arms showed depictions of skulls and half naked women. He had never done martial arts, he did however grow up with 3 brothers with an abusive alcoholic father on a council estate just outside the city. By day he worked on the building sites as a scaffolder and by night would hit the gym and sell a few drugs down the local. This guy was physical and had been fighting his entire life.

Right now, Darren was sinking, you could see him withering under the scaffolders aggression. He loomed over Darren making him capitulate through intimidation. I'm sure in Darren's arena he would easily have controlled this guy, but it wasn't his arena and the aggression had triggered some pretty powerful emotions in Darren that he wasn't ready for. We have all heard of the fight or flight response. Well there is a third to that called the freeze. That's what he did, the cocktail of chemicals charged around his body and his brain unable to find any similarity in what was happening shut down. His perceived experience of violence could find nothing to cling onto. All that physical training lost in a moment. The scaffolder lunged forward sinking a headbutt into Darren's face, he then grabbed him by the shirt and hit him with four or five swinging punches as Darren fell to the floor and tried to curl up in a ball totally overwhelmed by the ferocity of the attack. By the time help arrived the scaffolder was stamping on his head while holding the railings to get more purchase, spittle flew from his mouth as he shouted "cunt!" with every stamp. Darren was beaten, and the scaffolder didn't even bow.

This is not to say all martial arts are useless, far from it. But there is an illusion in certain circles that it can hold more prowess than perhaps it should. Oddly enough most good physical guys in security don't have a martial arts background, they just grew up scrapping. But if you can combine some good quality martial arts with an understanding of how street violence works, well that person becomes a dangerous beast.

Understanding the phycology of violence is critical and mostly overlooked by martial arts in general. That's why certain people like Geoff Thompson or Lee Morrison came to the fore. They brought with them an understanding of the fight. The first fight is the phycological one, and the master of that will almost certainly win the day. All bullies understand and use these tactics, so we need to learn them to. Remember Tyson in his heyday? He beat almost everyone without throwing a punch. His opponents would get into the ring already cowed and defeated just from the persona of the man. This is the power of mindset. That is the weapon that wins the fight. Yes, physical skills and prowess matter, but without the right mental approach your library of techniques are like a gun with no bullets.

Training Muay Thai.

My trip started on the Saturday night really with multiple phone calls to the local taxi companies asking for a short ride to the bus station at 5.45am. The answer was no, all except one turned me down flat and that one already had a booking at that time so could do six at the earliest. My coach and the first leg of my journey was due at 6.10am so I had to decline.

So that is how I found myself on a cold Sunday morning marching to the bus station dragging my luggage behind me.

The coach was functional, clean and on time and the first part of my journey was spent watching the beautiful English countryside disappear in and out of the ground mist that hung everywhere shrouding the fields and hedgerows and leaving everything sparkling with moisture when it did retreat. The sun came up on a crisp, sunny morning slowly gaining in height and taking the miles of motorway with it as it rose.

Heathrow Sunday morning 8.20am. The place is like a giant angry wasp's nest swarming with the urgency of each individual destination. Getting off the coach other passengers instantly surrounded me all being spewed onto the pavement from coaches and taxis along the drop off point. Some looked happy, others with a determined face steeled themselves and shot off into the airport.

As we were starting our journey others were finishing there's and bundling themselves back out onto UK soil. It was almost like a video game, some trundled past quite happy, others would hack away at your ankles with those wheelie suitcases until you moved while some just charged forward with an air of barely holding it together desperately trying to get out of the system. (This is the state I was in on arriving in Phuket, but at the start I just thought they were rude). You must make a snap decision as to which of these categories the person heading towards you fits into and react accordingly. I had plenty of time before my flight, so I inched my way into terminal 2 happily soaking up the atmosphere and watching the sea of humanity in all its forms race about me.

The first few hours flew by, checking in and going through security, drinking coffee, and just anticipating the journey ahead. Then on the board above my flight status changed. Delayed flashed angrily at me, blinking on and off. It was then replaced by a new time of 6pm UK time. Six hours later than planned. The wait began as myself and the rest of the disgruntled passengers started a long queue which snaked across the terminal floor, waiting for the £15 food voucher that would feed us until flight time. I took mine and headed straight back to a place I had noticed earlier. It offered a burger that sounded delicious. Aberdeen Angus steak with a shredded duck parfait, cheese, bacon, and a truffle sauce. I spent all the voucher on that burger and it was as good as it sounded. The wait seemed to last forever but eventually the time came to board. The flight was scheduled for just over 11 hrs and by flying cattle class to save money it was not a particularly comfortable experience. Don't ask me why but to pass the time I ended up watching

Notting Hill. You know the one with Julia Roberts and Hugh Grant. I put it down to altitude sickness.

Bangkok airport was a blur. We were met from the plane and then chased a petite Thai lady holding a sign across the airport to meet our new connecting flight. The Wai (Thai greeting) was everywhere and every official and employee we were passed to greeted us with the words "Sawatdi". Even with the haste in which we were being processed the polite formality was observed and I did my best to reciprocate, quite often fumbling with passport, booking forms and luggage it looked more like I was hitting myself in the head in some form of ritualised torture.

The thing I remember most about Bangkok was the wall of heat. You can read about it and you can see it on the television, but nothing prepares you for when you step out of the air-conditioned space into the outside world.

A short flight followed to Phuket. The beauty of the scenery from the plane window as we flew in was marred slightly by the fact that by now I smelled. 25 hours of flying and waiting had created levels of aromas that came from me that were beyond the power of wet wipes. I was aware of this and was embarrassed so I didn't enjoy the flight as much as I should have.

Stepping out into Phuket and the final part of my journey awaits. If I said earlier that Heathrow was an ants nest, then the front of the airport were sharks haranguing a giant fish bait ball. Cars and taxis where pulling out of everywhere and nobody was stopping for anybody. I was worn out and tired from the journey, my senses reeling from all that had happened and now crazy Thai taxi drivers in battered Toyotas were trying to mow me down. By this stage I'm not ashamed to admit I am a man on the edge. But my greatest challenge awaits. I need to get a taxi to the Chalong area where my hotel and all the fight camps are.

The taxi ride was THE most terrifying thing I have done in a long time. The driver was obviously very skilled as we had a good few near misses where I found myself pumping on the invisible brake pedal in the passenger footwell, but we had no accidents. Lanes existed but not to him and the general highway code seems to be see a gap a skateboard would fit into and force your car into it. I was struck on the journey by how normal and westernised it seemed to be one minute and then completely alien the next. We flew past a Tesco's on one side and on the other a scooter carrying five people, none of which had a helmet. Signs of the royal family are everywhere and large hoardings warning of the dangers of getting a tattoo of Buddha. Scooters are the preferred mode of transport weaving in and out of the traffic seemingly oblivious to the risks involved, dressed in shorts, t-shirts, and flip flops they would race into the traffic laden down with shopping and passengers to then be forced aside by the bigger vehicles.

We arrive at my hotel and the relief that after a total travelling time of 27 hours I am here. I pitch up take a shower then stroll round the many fight camps that are situated here. It is a fighter's paradise with everything on offer, but my head can't absorb it all tonight, so I book a session for the morning and sit quietly with a beer watching the small lizards wander about.

Day two and the training begins. It didn't quite work out how I wanted it to but started well. I woke up at about 4.30am. Just like that, wide awake. So, I went and sat by the pool listening to the chirruping of the frogs and insects as dawn approached. Finally, time for breakfast. The hotel starts serving at 9am so I won't be making that mistake again. Off to the convenience store later for some snacks to keep in my room. It was worth the wait and at 9am one of the smiling staff members brought me a strange version of breakfast. The sausages looked like they were made from luncheon meat and the bacon had the same shiny look as a toffee apple does. The first meal of the day was eaten while being serenaded by the sound of fist and shin hitting the Thai pads at the gym opposite, the trainer shouting instructions and the grunts of effort as people got there morning workout done before the sun got to hot.

After yet another shower I packed my training bag and began the short walk to the gym. On the way it was obvious what this part of Phuket is about, multiple gyms lined the streets while small groups of people sprinted backwards and forwards along the road and scooters buzzed by mostly ridden by fit young people in training gear. Little shack shops selling fresh fruit and smoothies were squeezed into every gap and a whole subculture has grown around the training gyms with chemists, tattooists, massage parlours and fight gear shops all trying to get you to spend your Baht with them.

So here I am at Tiger Muay Thai. After travelling 8000 miles over 27hrs I have finally made it. This morning I have signed up for a private 1 to 1 Muay Thai session followed by a grappling/mma class this afternoon. The front office was very polite, and I soon found myself sporting a brand-new pair of Tiger shorts.

My instructor greeted me with a warm smile and was very welcoming but looking at the lumps and scars on his shins and the callouses on his hands I knew that the smile masked a formidable fighter and even though quite short his movement was like a snake, very relaxed and slow and then a sudden burst of speed as he demonstrated a technique. The Thai instructors all seemed to be very cheerful and a sense of mischievousness runs through them. You can see the students that have been here a little while have built a rapport with them and there is a surprising amount of laughter all around the camp. It was time to start and while the mats were still wet from the constant mopping between classes I began to skip. The ropes are much heavier here so that combined with the slippery wet floor meant that I wasn't going to be impressing anyone soon. Some warm up jogging and stretching followed and then we began some very light pad work. We worked on my positioning and footwork and low-level combinations, all the time my instructor Sawat was correcting me with a smile, positioning my body and showing me the correct form. As the session wore on we started to up the pace and introduce some small combinations and fitness, 100 knees to the bag, 100 sit ups, repeat the kick, 1 2. And again 1 2. Again. This went on for some time and then just when I thought I was going to collapse from the exertion in the heat it was time for a one-minute rest and water. This was repeated throughout the session with constant tweaking to my technique and after only one hour I felt that I had improved. We ended the session with me gulping for air like a landed fish and covered in sweat. My instructor smiling as always rubbed me over with my towel and with a slight chuckle informed me "today was easy as first time, tomorrow harder". The walk back to the hotel took twice as long and I fell back into the shower then went for lunch as I had another class booked this afternoon.

Even though I had been training in striking arts for years, the heat and the humidity were kicking my arse. Combine that with the fact that as an instructor my own training had sometimes taken a back seat. Being honest, I'm getting older and I'm not as fit as I was. But enough of the excuses.

"Knee, Knee, Knee, cross, uppercut, right kick, go, go, go". His English is limited but he manages to get across what you need to do. Day two of training has begun. I woke up to the hottest day yet. My Casper the friendly ghost complexion was not going to like today, so I sat down for breakfast and then made my way to the gym. I had time to kill so mooched around the gym shop where I needed to pick up some fighter's oil on the request of the instructor. I also ended up buying a Tiger training vest, so I am now one of those guys. All the gear, no idea isn't it? It's time for class to start and here I stand looking like a walking advertising billboard for Tiger gym. After a light warm up my instructor asks for the oil, tells me to lay on my back and then proceeds to kneed and press the back of my calf's. The sensation was one of mild pain and discomfort as he worked my sore muscles from yesterday. It definitely had an effect and when I get up I could feel the backs of my legs tingling. Now it was time to apply the wraps, the instructor does this for you and already it is becoming a little ritual, almost a short meditation where your mind focuses in on the task ahead. Then it was time to start building the tempo of the training. As promised yesterday, today was harder. I was pushed more, and the heat made every effort so much more draining.

But this was why I was here. To immerse myself in the culture and the heritage of Thailand. We in the UK have Football as a national sport. In Thailand Thai boxing is everywhere. Little kids sit at the curb side conditioning their shins with old bottles filled with sand. I wanted to see what the country was like and was lucky enough to experience some great moments as well as training every day. I was blessed by a monk at the top of a mountain. I couldn't touch him, but he swished a leafy branch around my head and mumbled some sort of chant and then I was presented with a blessing in the guise of a rope wristband. This now sits in my gym reminding me of that time. Martial arts have given me so much and I often wonder how my life would have ended up without it.

My first competition.

I had been doing traditional Karate for a while and had reached green belt. It was time to test my prowess and see how I would do. This was a small area event based at Yate leisure centre. The main hall was kitted out with four matted fighting areas. All around me were Karateka in there crisp white Gi's. Milling around were the officials, they looked very professional in their dark blazers, ties, and perfectly ironed dress trousers. It was a strange feeling as I nervously looked around the room to see if I could spot likely opponents. I would only be fighting people of my own standard so anyone green or below. I scanned the room and notice everyone was doing similar.

The way these competitions are set up means there is a lot of down time. You are expected to sign in and register first thing in the morning and then you may have to wait around most of the day for your fight. And other than a loose schedule posted up you had no idea when it would be your turn so trying to keep stretched and warm was a balancing act. Too much and you would burn out long before your fight, to little and you would be stiff and slow and run a high risk of injuring yourself.

The fighting began, and the groups were called to the areas. Points karate sparring is nothing like a fight you see on a Saturday night. It is a cat and mouse game of poise, precision, and timing. I watched as the two guys in the centre of the mats bounced up and down in front of each other just out of range. Then one would launch an attack with a loud Kai! If it landed the referee would stop the fight by yelling "Yame" and award the point. An Ippon was what you were after. That was awarded for what would have been a finishing blow if you had followed through with the strike. At the end of the bout the combatants would bow to each other and the points would be tallied up.

I sat around the edge of the fighting area. My group had been called. We each formed a line along the edge of the mats and knelt until it was our turn. I watched as the fights progressed, nervous about how I would perform. My legs were slowly starting to seize up underneath me. Finally, I was called and got up to take my place. In traditional Karate you get given a belt to wear for the fight and as I was handed mine I realised my hands were shaking so much I couldn't do it up. Adrenaline had kicked in and I had no clue. This had never happened before, and no-one had warned me. I thought I was a coward as my hands were shaking. I stood there embarrassed as my instructor tied the knot on my belt for me and pushed me onto the mats. This effect was something I would learn about over the years but at that point it had never been mentioned and no-one had told me that a lot of the moves I thought I could do I would never be able to pull off due to my body kicking in to its fight or flight response. It was only years later when Geoff Thompson came on the scene and openly talked about these things did I realise that my reaction was normal, and everyone goes through it.

Old school surgery.

Whack! I had just taken a full-on straight punch to the bridge of the nose. The gloves we were wearing had a tiny amount of padding on them and suggested protection more than offered any. I staggered back, but the fight was still on, so I went forward again trying to land my shots. We continued back and forth through the round as blood dripped freely from my nostrils until time was called. We bowed, shook hands, and gave each other a hug. Its funny have ten seconds ago we were trying to hurt one another but now its over there is no animosity. That's how it is most of the time and contrary to what some people believe we don't hate each other we just have this strange compulsion to find out who is better.

I looked in the mirror and took the rolled-up toilet paper away from my nose. The blood had more or less stopped but my nose had been pushed across my face and I stared at the monstrosity looking back. We were in a karate class in the early nineties and the other students looked at me in a mixture of horror and fascination. My instructor at the time, a former European champion who had lived and trained in Japan gave it a cursory inspection and asked if I wanted it sorted. Sensei was and still is a formidable force of nature and his presence and strength of will is probably what he is best known for. I was lucky that I got to spend the years I did under his tutelage and his guidance and teachings have been invaluable.

"Lie down" he said. So right there in the middle of the dojo I led down on the mats. The other students gathered round in a semi-circle peering down at me. My instructor stood over me and reaching down put a hand either side of my nose and with a loud cracking noise yanked it back across my face. The other students pulled faces and winced and a fresh wave of pain shot through my head. My instructor stood up and reached down a hand to help me up. This time when I looked in the mirror my nose and eyes were already swelling but my nose once again, was straight. The class was called to order and the sparring resumed as if nothing had happened.

I have to say that it was days like these that helped to discipline my mind. Training the body is easy, training the mind is the difficult job. Martial arts are a great way of doing that. I remember once breaking my hand in a fight and when I told my coach between rounds what had happened his response was "fucking kick him then".

12: You shouldn't laugh, but.......

Always keep a skinhead handy.

While working a pub with my mate Matty we worked out this interesting way to modify the behaviour of rowdy punters. This was a city centre bar that was very popular as a warm up venue, meaning it got very busy between ten and midnight but would then die off as the customers would move on to the late clubs. The trendy guys and girls with there finger on the pulse of the latest go to club would congregate at ours and then move on. This brought the groups of lads as wherever you have a lot of young, beautiful women wearing very little you would always get men to follow them. We were the only two doormen working and sometimes we could have a busy bar of over two hundred people. One of our locals that drank there every weekend was a monster of a man, just shy of seven feet with a shaved head covered in tattoos and those spiky lip things. He was actually a really nice guy but looked formidable. He also had a strange sense of humour and didn't mind us using him to set an example. Whenever a group got to much we would give the signal and our giant friend would make a bit of a scene. One of us would go over and give him the talking too. He would become cowed and loudly exclaim that he wanted no trouble with us, he had heard about us and would behave. The rowdy groups would see this and think to themselves those doormen must be something special and calm it down. Surprisingly, our plan worked most of the time.

When you can't stop peeing.

Summer was here and with it came the drunken punters hanging around and the groups of people that would aimlessly walk around the streets all night. I'm on my door, it's a quiet night for us and I am daydreaming about finishing and getting to bed. Across the road from the entrance are some allocated parking spaces and in one of those spaces was the club owner's car. Unfortunately, also occupying the parking space was a drunk guy swaying slightly. His belt and the flies of his jeans were undone, and he held his penis in his hand while he aimed a steady flow of urine up the side of the boss's car. I marched across the street and told him to stop pissing on it. He replied with" mate, you know you can't stop once you've started". With that response I shoved him hard. I must have pushed a little harder than I meant to and as he was also a little drunk he went sailing up into the air, cock still in hand. Piss drew a wide arc through the air in a human version of a Catherine wheel. He ended up on his butt covered in his own wee. But he did stop peeing. He grumbled and moaned and complained that I shouldn't have done that, but I knew just how lucky he was. In the next parking space along was my colleagues new BMW. That was his pride and joy and I can only imagine what he would have done if he had found this idiot pissing on his car. For weeks after this guy would appear in the doorway of some of the bars on our street. He would just stand there and stare at me. He never did anything, and I never could figure out if he was trying to intimidate me or just liked standing alone in the street. Eventually I saw him less and less. I guess he got over it.

Cupped on gay night.

I was head doorman at this particular venue for a number of years and once a month it ran a gay night. The monthly promotion was incredibly successful, and the club would be packed from the moment we opened. On these nights we had a long queue of people lined up waiting for us to open the doors. The club would soon fill to bursting and would stay that way for the rest of the evening. Mostly these nights were drama free. Occasionally the lesbians would have a punch up but mostly it was a party atmosphere as the 80's cheese blared out. Most of our work came at the front door. Usually our club ran drum and bass nights and was a place where local promoters would book the night and bring their friends to mc on the mike. It was a very different crowd to what we had on these evenings. Quite often our regular type of punter would try to get in. Despite the fact this night was widely advertised and happened every month we would still get the wannabe gangsters coming up wanting to get in not realising what they were getting in to. We would have to politely try and tell them that what was going on inside the club was not what they were expecting. Its not that they weren't welcome as you didn't have to be gay to attend its just that when the lad you are explaining this to replies with "its allright bruv, I ain't got no beef with fags" you just sort of know that won't end well. There were four of us working this particular night and this was maybe our second or third of these promotions. We were all still getting used to each other. At this venue we had a scheduled walk round and toilet check every thirty minutes. Normal rules didn't apply, and the men's room would be empty as everyone would crowd into the ladies. As it was a new promotion for us and a very popular one I decided to take charge of the interior checks initially.

It was that time again, I left the very busy door and started to push my way through the crowds. If you have never seen a gay night in full swing it is quite the experience. Six feet plus guys teetered around in shiny boob tubes, their chest hair curling over the top. Men snogged and fondled each other in the shadows. Almost everyone on the dancefloor was bare chested and knew all the latest choreographed dance moves. As I pushed my way through the stifling crowds I suddenly felt a hand lightly cup my balls. I spun round to see a group of middle aged guys all sniggering like schoolgirls. I was furious and demanded to know who did that. They all shrugged and held up their hands in the most unconvincing show of innocence I had ever seen. "If I find out which one of you did that I am going to knock them the fuck out". I ranted at the group. I spun on my heels and marched straight back to the safety of the front door. In my gruffest no-nonsense voice, I demanded that someone else needed to go and do the checks and that from now on I would no longer go inside unless there was a problem. The guys asked me what had happened, I declined to say. Sensing that I was uncomfortable the guys kept asking and asking, refusing to let it drop. Eventually they wore me down and I snapped. "I was cupped" I said. If I was expecting sympathy I was wrong. The guys immediately burst into laughter and thought this was the funniest thing all night, they proceeded to take the piss out of me for the rest of the shift. But it didn't end there. Every single time the promotion was on someone would remind me of the cupping incident.

The beard rule.

The club had an over 25 policy. If you looked under 25 you would be asked for ID. This is normal in clubland and most people are aware of it and yet still some people turn up with none. This was the case with this young lady. The club entrance was set up so the queue went down the side of the building and didn't snake into the road. We would have two security at the head of the queue checking Id's. At that point the customers would be filtered either into the club or past the barriers and back into the street if they were refused. Two ladies were next in the line and one of them offered forward a passport, the other lady said she had forgot hers. I explained the 25 rule and explained that she would need to get some form of ID for us to let her in. She did look over 18 but that was the policy of the club. Both her and her friend were syphoned off from the queue where they stood and loitered. Next up was a gentleman that also had no id. "that's fine" I said, "go on in". The young ladies from a moment ago chirped up at this point asking why he was allowed in. I replied, "because he has a beard". He obviously looked over 25 and was sporting a full-on beard. I explained to the ladies that in this instance that was proof enough. I then turned back to the line as the ladies wandered off. 15 minutes later the ladies were back and again took their place in the queue. When I saw them I burst out laughing. The young lady without ID had gone to the corner shop and brought a marker pen. She had then drawn a beard on herself and stood before me with a full dark beard on her face. We had to let her in after that.

The human fireball.

This bar is for the pretty people, situated on a long straight strip of road that was in fashion the punters would move up and down it frequenting all the bars to be seen in. We were one of those. To get in you had to go through a set of revolving doors where door staff and management would look you over to see if you made the grade before letting you pass. This was an affluent 25-40 something crowd that dressed well and was blessed with good genes. Anyone not fitting the description was discouraged from entering. You would often hear the manager in your earpiece telling you who was good looking enough to get in and who wasn't. The bar sold cocktails and the staff would race backwards and forwards spinning the bottles and throwing them in the air only to catch them again, and with a flourish pour the liquid into a shaker. The glass would be finished with a sugar frosting or a dusting of fruit and then the whole thing would be presented to the customer as a reward for watching the performance.

I was stood on my usual perch a few steps up the spiral staircase. From there I could oversee the bar and floor area. From my vantage point I could scan across the room without making unnecessary eye contact with people. At the bar were a small group of young men and as young men do they were egging each other on to order the most outrageous cocktails we supplied. The drink they ordered was placed in front of them as the barman grandly waved the lighter around as if performing a magic trick. He then swept it across the top of the glass as the alcohol caught fire and erupted in flames. With his mates egging him on the young man picked up the still flaming drink and to the chants of "down it" he tilted his head back and drank the burning liquid. In his haste he over tilted the glass and the fiery liquid sloshed over the rim and down the front of him setting his shirt alight. His mates screamed in delight as he pulled his shirt off his back threw it to the floor stamping out the last of the flames. They all found this highly amusing and I must admit I was enjoying the spectacle as well when my earpiece went off. It was the manager telling me that the guy can't stay in the bar bare chested and I was to escort him out. Well that hardly seemed fair as it was technically us that set him on fire so instead of kicking him out we rummaged in the storeroom and found some free promotional t-shirts and gave him one of them. All the while the lads were daring each other to do another one.

Every book needs a car chase.

I'm stood on the door, it's a slow Friday night. The club is less than half full and the customers that are coming in are few and far between. I'm stood with my mate and on nights like this passing time is the name of the game. Usually it will involve ripping the piss out of each other, dark humour and maybe a bit of teasing the punters. Minutes feel like hours and the shift seems never ending. Our door for tonight opens straight out onto the street. Along our row are a series of bars which disappears around the corner towards the centre. We get a lot of through traffic and the taxis use the street as a rat run to avoid the ever-worsening Bristol road systems.

We are stood leaning against the wall trying to think of new insults to hurl at one another when the sound of something like a lawnmower reaches us. The machine is not happy, and you can hear it at the top of its revs. It's getting louder and we can now here shouting and laughing. Around the corner hurtles a mobility scooter, perhaps hurtle is the wrong word. It is one of those burgundy ones with the basket on the front. On it are four young men and they are driving it flat out along the road. They are all clinging preciously to one another as they laugh and zig-zag from side to side. As they draw alongside us another noise reaches our ears. This time it is the sound of horse's hooves hitting the pavement as round the corner comes a female mounted Police officer giving chase. The mobility scooter rattles passed closely followed by the police horse. Up close these things are massive and it was gaining with every stride. They both disappeared from view and I have no idea how it ended, but it did cheer up an otherwise uneventful shift.

Nipple tassels.

The club is hidden down a side street just off the main drag. Opposite us is one of the UK's most famous gay bars. The road that separates us is narrow and we had a well-established working relationship with them. Our firm also ran the door there so if it was required we would lend a hand. With me during this time was Dan the young lad I had mentioned before, and this kind of scene was something of an eyeopener for him.

The manager across the street was an interesting guy. He was in his mid-forties and spreading just a little around the middle. He stood about 5'8 and had medium length dark hair and wore glasses. In fact, he looked just like your average joe and family man. But that was on Friday's. On Saturdays the caterpillar would become the butterfly and he would lather on the make-up, wear a tiara, and waft a big feather fan around as he shimmied from group to group. He spoke with an incredibly camp manner and accentuated his feminine traits, which was in complete contrast to Fridays deep baritone. It was almost like he had two personalities and the Saturday side of him was a little flamboyant to say the least.

On the quieter moments or when they wanted change or ice he would come over to our door .This made our young Dan just a little nervous and he really didn't know how to handle the situation which in the managers eyes just fanned the flames and encouraged him to wind Dan up. Then one evening it reached its zenith when he sashayed across the road heading straight for us. He had a glittery tight top on which exposed both his muffin top and hairy shoulders. Tonight, in his hand he had a wand with a star on the end and as he approached he made a beeline for Dan. As per usual he went bright red and started to stutter his words. As his uncomfortableness grew the manager reached down and grabbed the bottom of his glittery top. While maintaining solid eye contact he lifted his top exposing a pair of nipple tassels clamped to his greying chest. He then started to swing them back and forth in some obscene dance as he tried to rub them on Dan. Of course, it goes without saying the rest of us found the whole thing highly amusing.

Challenge excepted.

We are backstage, and the concert is in full swing. The band started in the seventies and have been turning out music ever since. They peaked in the mid-eighties but still had a loyal and vocal fanbase. Every year they would tour and every year they would come to our venue to roll out the greatest hits to thunderous applause and a few new songs that were greeted with apathy. The had been around so long the guitarists son was in the support band and they were now flitting between the green room and the tour bus.

The band had a well-rehearsed procedure for leaving venues. The moment they finished the encore they would grab towels and dressing gowns from the waiting crew and be escorted to the nearest exit where the bus would be waiting. They would then file onto the bus and disappear into the night. The aim was to get this done before the fans could get out and around the building to ask for photos and signatures.

As we waited for the end of there set we were having some banter with the support group. One of the things they were joking about was the size of Steve. Steve is a mountain of a man at 6'4 and easily 30 stone. Gold chains hung around where his neck should have been, and more gold lay around his chunky forearms. He moved like a cruise ship, whenever the radio called he would go into this funny speed walk. He never ran but would propel himself along at a determined gait.

Anyway, as the banter escalated a bet was placed. Can Steve squeeze into the tour bus toilet? As the band played behind us we slipped out the doors giggling like kids and got the driver to open the door. With a last look to make sure none of the venue management were looking we piled onto the bus. It was time to earn the bet and the door to the cramped cubicle was opened. This was one of those luxury buses with leather everything and large flat screens. It looked just like a posh hotel room on wheels. The years of drug and alcohol abuse were now just part of the bands folklore and comfort was the priority. Even so the cubicle was incredibly tight. I stepped in and tried it for size. I'm not small guy and even at my size it was a squeeze. Now it was Steve's turn and with much cheering from the band he began to inch sideways into the space. As he crabbed in he had to hold his girth with his hands. He had pretty much wedged himself in but there was no way he could turn around or sit down. Now it was time to close the door. Imagine trying to zip up the lid of a thirty stone overstuffed suitcase. Hands were used to try to push the last bits of Steve in as the door was inched towards closing. All the while we are laughing like children as the driver looks on shaking his head. With a last determined push, we close the door with a cheer. In the silence that followed all you could hear was the sound of heavy breathing from the exertion and Steve's muffled voice pleading to be let out.

Where for art thou?

It is one of those glorious summer days, the sun is shining with a clear blue sky and a wisp of a breeze occasionally brings respite to the heat. We are at a festival again. This is a smaller local festival, maybe two thousand people or so. This means that our firm have the full security contract which is good because it means the gang get to meet up. One of the best things about these sorts of jobs was that you got to see the old faces and have a right laugh. Remember that we all had our own bars and clubs to manage every weekend, so this was an opportunity to get together and people would come from across the country. As always, the day started the same way, a bunch of oversized, ugly lads would squeeze into a small family car with much cussing and calling each other names. There would need to be a garage stop on the way and the men in black would force themselves out of the car to stock up on red bull and sausage rolls.

On arriving on site more name calling and piss taking. This by the way is a bonding ritual and is a necessary part of the process. Next would come the greetings, and here's a secret for you. The way the guy shakes your hand tells you what they really think of you. First is the nod of acknowledgment, maybe even a mumbled "alright". This means you're ok, but I don't really rate you. Next is the one handed formal shake. This usually means I have been forced into doing this and although I think your ok I would have rather done the nod. Then comes the two-handed grasp, I'm pleased to see you and I think you're a good guy. Finally, the manly shake and hug. The hands clasp together, and both lean into a shoulder bump and a backslap. This is the sign of ultimate acceptance. You don't get one of these unless you have earned it and no doorman worth his salt would give you this greeting unless he meant it.

Greetings over and the brief given we move out to our positions, so the day could start. One of the younger lads excitedly asked if we had seen the paramedics that were working? We knew he didn't mean them both, he meant the pretty one with the long dark hair who even in her green overalls looked very womanly in all the right places. Of course we had noticed her! As we got ready to open the site he continued to mention her and would wistfully glance repeatedly at the ambulance parked up in the corner of the site. What you should never do is show emotion or weakness to your colleagues on a long shift. This is an open invitation to have the mickey taken out of you for the rest of the day. As the day wore on the medical guys would wander around stopping and chatting to people, at this point they had no medical issues to deal with so were just filling time. As they came to the gate you could see the young lad blushing and getting embarrassed. This only made it worse, so we dropped lots of loaded sentences into the conversation. The lady paramedic seemed to know what was going on and didn't seem to mind. The day carried on with us teasing him, him taking shy looks at her and calling us arseholes, and her seemingly interested in him. Enough was enough and it was time for Cupid to arrive in the shape of a twenty stone security guard. Getting bored of all the talk and no action he marched up to the young lady and uttered those immortal words "My mate fancies you". We are all in stitches as he points towards our young mate who is recoiling in horror. She laughs and smiles and mumbles something in Cupids ear. "He seems cute" she giggled.

More time went past and we all got tired as neither one of them was going to make the first move. So, we got together and hatched a plan. We slowly circled our young friend and, on the signal, we pounced. We grabbed hold of him and pinned him to the ground as he squirmed and fought to get away. Between us we must have weighed in at around seventy stone and as we each grabbed an arm and a leg and lifted him bodily into the air. He is pleading with us by now, begging us to put him down. Punters watch in fascination as we manhandle our colleague across the event field towards the first aid tent. As they see us coming the paramedics come out to stare, the young ladies mouth flew open and her hand reached to cover it as she watched us dump our young friend on the ground at her feet. "He's got something to ask you" we said. He is lying on the ground his face bright red and his is hissing dire consequences at us. The things he is threatening us with should not reach a lady's ears so a quick nudge with a boot is administered to bring him into line. "Alright!" he yells. "Enough". He takes a deep breath and with eyes firmly fixed on the floor he asks her out on a date. She calls us all bullies and accepts. Our little group give out a cheer and we wander back to the job we are supposed to be doing.

13: After

The straw that broke the camel's back.

This incident is why I never renewed my badge. It also highlights some of the problems we as door supervisors face night after night with low pay and very little thanks for what we do. I honestly believe that this was the last of my nine lives and my luck was coming to an end. I also cannot understand the decision that was reached regards punishing this person. If I was going to deal with such violence I stupidly expected the backing of our legal system. How wrong I was.

I am on my usual door. It's another drum and bass night and the clientele are mostly scrotes. Gang culture and drugs are rife and anyone coming into this environment unaware are just going to become victims. And that is exactly what happened. Two university kids, white upper middle-class and sheltered were out and wanted something urban and edgy. Like a lot of students let lose in the big city, alone and with money for the first time they often bite off more than they can chew. One of the crews saw these pair and realised they were vulnerable. So, he sidled up alongside them and tried to steal from the girl's bag. She noticed this and confronted the thief. The boyfriend quick to defend her stepped in and demanded he give the phone back. The thief calmly told him he would stab him if they didn't fuck off. The students not knowing what to do came and spoke to me explaining what had happened. The described the lad. Black, about 5"10, maybe 25 years old with a tattoo on the side of his neck. He was wearing a baseball cap, red jacket, and grey joggers. He was easy to find so I walked him towards the hallway away from the noise to speak to him. He saw the students and began yelling threats at them. I grabbed his arm to lead him away and he swung a wide punch at my head. I easily avoided the shot but before I could land one of my own he was trying to swing more. I wrapped him up and dragged him to the front door where I bundled him out into the street, pushing him away from me out of punching range. My colleagues and I stood there forming a solid wall across the door denying him entry or attack. He threatened us and yelled and then stormed off. Good I thought, at least he is gone. But I was wrong. He had gone around the corner and found an empty bottle. He then came back and ran at me swinging the bottle at my head. I threw up my arm, flinching away from the threat as the bottle impacted squarely on my arm in line with my temple. He then dropped the bottle and ran. Fortunately for me there were two police officers on patrol nearby and gave chase. They also radioed for back up and in a very short amount of time more officers arrived. They were needed as the thief was brought down by a female officer, who performed a great WWE style forearm smash, but it took six of them to hold him. He assaulted several of them while he was being detained and put up quite a fight. I was lucky to still be in one piece as his intention had been to hurt me. I continued with the night and after I finished the shift I drove to the police station where I gave a statement and spent two hours of my life I will never get back. They said they would be in touch.

The next day, later in the afternoon I am working a small festival when my phone goes. It's quiet and I'm out the way so I answer it. It's a lady from the police who informs me of the thief's fate. I could have yelled at her as she explained the poor darling had been let off with a caution as it was his first offence and he was very sorry. Bear in mind he had stolen, then threatened to stab someone, then assaulted me, then assaulted me again with a bottle and then assaulted a number of police officers while resisting arrest all on camera with multiple witnesses. I was fuming and still feel very let down by the system. I'm pretty sure they wouldn't have been so lenient and given me a caution if I had tried to bottle someone.

Costs.

Everything has a cost, and this is no exception, physically my hands are battered and broken. Most of my fingers are misshapen and deformed. Knuckles and skin calloused and scarred. The little finger on my right hand was so badly damaged where it wasn't just broken but shattered that we seriously discussed amputating it for a while. My nose has been broken three times and now is like a piece of play-do it is so malleable. That was actually to my advantage as after the first time in happened whilst training Karate my eyes never watered again whist being punched in the nose, however I did suffer from sinus problems for many years. I have a few scars dotted around my body from bottles, bats and other tokens of affection that people would offer, and I ache almost all of the time, but I have been very lucky that that is the extent of my injuries.

Psychologically I have been affected. I have seen some horrible things and been involved in and witness to levels of violence that are very unhealthy for the mind. Seeing the worst of humanity leaves a stain on your soul that is hard to remove and at the end I was having violent thoughts towards everybody. Just as a dentist will check out your teeth when you meet as that's his default setting and job, and the brickie will walk down the street and say to himself that walls not plum. I found myself lining everyone up. I would be in the supermarket buying a loaf of bread and I would have visualised knocking the cashier unconscious with a short hook just in case she got lippy. I would talk to the neighbours with my chin tucked in in case he tried to headbutt me. Not that he ever did. Every conversation I had at that time was superimposed with how I would physically dominate the situation should it call for it no matter if it was buying chips or chatting about the weather. I had become that person who was forever expecting the worst. And the violence I had lived with so long had become hardwired into my brain. I only realised what that had done to me once I stopped working the doors and anybody who has never been around that level of violence for that length of time will never understand.

It's not all drunk punters.

It has been a great pleasure to have met some incredible people through this work. Celebrities, pop stars, royalty, sporting heroes' but its not just interesting people I was fortunate enough to meet.

Today we are looking after a car show with a difference. The show is in the grounds of a very expensive private school and the collection on show would include cars worth millions, cars belonging to Hollywood movie stars and vehicles that have been used on the big screen. This was big boy's toys at its most extravagant and you needed deep pockets to own these kinds of vehicles. Part of our remit was safely getting all the cars and owners onto the site and to the allocated positions we had for them. Suddenly my radio goes in my ear and I am informed I am required on the green. I make my way over to be told a helicopter with a VIP on-board will be arriving any minute and my job is to land it. Now I have seen those guys with earmuffs and table tennis bats on the TV but had zero knowledge of what I was supposed to do. As the chopper approached I started waving my arms and pacing backwards having little clue at what I was doing but thoroughly enjoying the moment. The helicopter landed safely, and we escorted the VIP away as the rotor blades picked up speed and lifted the chopper back into the sky.

Speaking of cars, I was also fortunate to spend the night looking after the worlds fastest car a few years ago. Unfortunately, it was on a trailer, so I never got to see it in action but just being close to such a magnificent piece of engineering was a rare privilege.

I'm chatting to the boss and he says how do you feel about looking after a formula 1 car. "great" I said little knowing what I was agreeing too. One of the clubs on Park Street was running a promotion with the energy drink Red Bull, you know the one that gives you wings. So as part of the deal last years Red Bull car would be parked up outside the front of the club for the course of the night. The only thing between it and the drunken Saturday night hordes was some rope, myself and Alex a big 6'8 guy with shovel hands and a filthy sense of humour. As you can imagine the car created a lot of buzz and loads of people wanted to get in it to have photos taken. Of course, that was not allowed and it turned into quite a long night, made worse by the fact that neither Alex nor I could sit in the bloody thing either as we were too big.

A new life.

My passion is now teaching, and I am grateful that I am in the privileged position where I can do that. Watching others progress and become better people or become trained and qualified to feed their family or overcoming fear and anxiety is an amazing feeling. Waking up every morning looking forward to hopefully making a difference in the world means a lot.

A chance meeting with a posh kid.

Around ten years ago my phone rang as I was walking down the street. A very softly spoken voice introduced themselves as Adam and asked if he could have a moment of my time. He asked if I would be interested in working with him on a charity project of his. We agreed to meet at a café in Taunton a few days later.

I am sat watching the world go by at the café. As the clock ticks it's way round to the meeting time a guy approaches me. He is young and has a round face with red cheeks, he is constantly pushing his fringe to one side with one hand while the other clasps a satchel type bag. He offers a hand and smiles while we get through the pleasantries.

Adams family story is a terrible one and I sat there transfixed, horrified, and saddened as the details of what happened unfolded. In 2005 Adams brother Lloyd was walking home from a party with a few friends when they were attacked by another group of males. The group began to beat them, and Lloyd was hit over the head with a wooden post and then beaten and kicked on the floor. He died at the scene the day before his eighteenth birthday.

Adam felt he needed to do something and began to form the charity Stand Against Violence and this is where I come in. He explained that he would like for me to work with them delivering self-defence workshops. As I sat there drinking my coffee trying to comprehend even a little bit of what he and his family must have gone through he mapped out his plan. He said that he wanted to build an organisation that travelled the UK delivering the message of anti-violence. Through knowledge and education, he hoped to reach out to our youth and let them know of the dangers and consequences. Using Lloyd's story, he intended to connect with schools and organisations and try to change our world for the better. I listened to his grand plan and wondered if this fresh faced, softly spoken middle class kid could build such a thing, remember at this time it was in its infancy and hadn't outgrown the town of Taunton.

I really like the idea and ethos behind the charity and even though I wasn't sure it would go anywhere I readily agreed to be a part of it. Here we are ten years later, and I am really glad I did. Turns out that softly spoken voice hides a man of great integrity and mental fortitude. Over the years I have seen the charity grow to achieve great things, the things he talked about all those years ago continue to come to fruition and I have built a programme for schools for the charity that we continue to deliver to schools across the UK. In fact, we have expanded so much I have had to train other instructors to help share the message.

Two days before writing this I was delivering self-defence to an inner-city girl's school. Fourteen-year-old young ladies of many races and religions learned some basic fundamentals of staying safe over the course of the day. I Know that what we do is a positive and if it only helps one teenager make the right decision then it's all worth it.

Defence against what?

I wear many hats now with my training and teaching and I often get asked to deliver bespoke training packages for businesses and groups. The phone rang at it was the owner of a bailiff company I sometimes do some work for. He had a question for me.

How would you defend yourself against a chainsaw? He was ringing as during the work they do they sometimes come into contact with members of the travelling community. The day before had been one of those days for them. The company had been hired to perform an eviction from private land. So, they had gathered together some staff members, jumped into the trucks, and drove across country as the dawn rose around them. They were due to arrive for 8am and had been assured that the local police would meet them at the camp at that time. They arrived and there were no police, and what was worse the travellers were instantly hostile. Threats were shouted, and violence hung in the morning mist. From one of the caravans came a large man wielding a chainsaw. He ran at the team, chainsaw held high yelling as he came. As he did this, other men started to appear with makeshift weapons. The team were forced to withdraw to the trucks where they made a hasty escape down the muddy dirt track. This all happened in a farmer's field in rural middle England at 8am on a misty spring morning. I couldn't really think of an answer that was workable and legal.

I am still involved in the security world and deliver the training required to get the badge to work and offer professional consultation. I teach martial arts and self-defence and deliver conflict management and assertiveness training. I am lucky to still be able to train and teach and as we move into the modern age and my latest challenge is learning the technology required to bring martial arts teaching into the future. Blogs, online courses, and

YouTube are making the world of martial arts far more accessible and I am enjoying the challenge of keeping up. Would I ever go back to frontline work? Well, you can never say never but the money has dropped out the bottom and the risks increase year on year, also I am getting old.

But I do miss the excitement and my brothers in arms.

Printed in Poland
by Amazon Fulfillment
Poland Sp. z o.o., Wrocław